D0344576

Learning in Depth

Learning in Depth

A Simple Innovation That Can Transform Schooling

KIERAN EGAN

The University of Chicago Press   Chicago and London

KIERAN EGAN is a professor of education at Simon Fraser University. He is also a winner of the Grawemeyer Award in Education, a Kappa Delta Pi Laureate, an American Educational Research Association Fellow, a foreign associate member of the National Academy of Education, a Fellow of the Royal Society of Canada, Director of the Centre for Imaginative Education, and a Canada Research Chair in Cognitive Development and the Curriculum.

The University of Chicago Press, Chicago 60637
The University of Chicago Press, Ltd., London
© 2010 by Kieran Egan
All rights reserved. Published 2010
Printed in the United States of America

19 18 17 16 15 14 13 12 11 10   1 2 3 4 5

ISBN-13: 978-0-226-19043-3 (cloth)
ISBN-10: 0-226-19043-9 (cloth)

Library of Congress Cataloging-in-Publication Data

Egan, Kieran.
  Learning in Depth : a simple innovation that can transform schooling /
  Kieran Egan.
    p. cm.
  Includes bibliographical references.
  ISBN-13: 978-0-226-19043-3 (cloth: alk. paper)
  ISBN-10: 0-226-19043-9 (cloth: alk. paper)
  1. Learning in Depth (Program) 2. Educational innovations. 3. Curriculum change. 4. Active learning. 5. Research. 6. Knowledge, Theory of. I. Title
  LB1027.E4135 2010
  371.2'07—dc22
                                           2010011679

♾ The paper used in this publication meets the minimum requirements of the American National Standard for Information Sciences—Permanence of Paper for Printed Library Materials, ANSI Z39.48-1992.

Contents

Acknowledgments

I am grateful for the helpful criticism given to drafts of this book by my colleagues in the Imaginative Education Research Group at Simon Fraser University in Canada. I am particularly grateful to Gillian Judson, Kym Stewart, Tannis Calder, and Krystina Madej for reading the manuscript and making incisive criticisms and suggestions for improving it. I gained a lot of helpful suggestions from the great students in Simon Fraser University's Imaginative Education M.Ed. cohorts, with particular thanks for specific suggestions to Hannah Bernardino, Karen Faryna, Lili Ge, Laura Kenny, Kangja Lee, Sean McLaughlin, Bratislav Mladenovic, Nancy Palejko, Sylvia Showler, Emily White, Sharon Widdows, Erica Zaiser, "J. O." Eriksson, David Futter, Patricia Goodson, Lezley Hiebert, Dennis Kraft, Jenifer Morrison, Sara Neall, Stacey Soffel, Todd Stewart-Rinier, Andy Sundahl, Paul Wright, Dmitri Zebroff, and Yvan Zebroff. During classes with these teachers/students I first mentioned the Learning in Depth idea, and Linda Holmes and David Futter decided to give it a go in their own classrooms, producing the first implementations of the idea. I am most grateful for their ingenuity and commitment in putting the idea into practice, for providing me with the encouragement to keep writing the book as a result of their wonderfully successful work with the first groups of LiDKids, and for providing their students with an enriching experience.

Bob Dunton, principal of the remarkable Corbett Charter School, and the impressive teachers of Corbett have raised questions, concerns, and ideas that have made this book more clear and practical than it might otherwise have been. Also their careful planning for an extensive implementation has been both encouraging and enlightening; to see superbly professional teachers taking an idea and articulating it into the complex context of their classrooms' daily life has been inspiring. Craig Worthing and the teachers of Anderson Elementary School, Richmond, B.C., were really helpful in the process of thinking through many of the potential practical and theoretical problems with the proposal. Hugh Burke, headmaster of Meadowridge School in Maple Ridge, B.C., was generous with his time and insights, as was Di Fleming, director of Accelerated Knowledge Technologies Pty Ltd., Melbourne, Australia. Laurie Anderson, acting superintendent, Vancouver School Board, gave me some helpful insights into administrators' views of the proposal, and support in locating schools interested in implementing LiD, as did Dr. Fred Renihan, ex-superintendent of the Surrey School Board. Dr. Geoff Madoc-Jones, coordinator of the Ed.D. program in the Faculty of Education, Simon Fraser University, and Dr. Jean Warburton both have contributed helpful insights into how the program might work. I am grateful also for specific help from Drs. Robin Barrow, Heesoon Bai, Allan MacKinnon, and Don McLeod of SFU's Faculty of Education; Dr. Gadi Alexander of Ben Gurion University; Isabelle Eaton, researcher with the Canadian Council on Learning; Teresa Martin, administrative coordinator of the IERG; Melanie Young and Stacey Makortoff, research assistants on the LiD project; and also from Pamela Thomas and Susanna Egan. I received many insightful suggestions on both form and content from Catherine Egan.

During the writing of this book I have been the grateful beneficiary of a grant from the Social Sciences and Humanities Research Council of Canada.

Important in improving the book in more ways than I can enumerate has been Elizabeth Branch Dyson of the University of Chicago Press. The book appears in its current form—from a number of its structural features down to details of the content and not least as a part of Chicago's list—due to her commitment, good advice, many suggestions for improvement, good humor, and having more of the virtues of a good editor than any author has a right to expect. I am immensely grateful to her, and, should the book lead to implementations of the Learning in Depth program, the expertise of children who may take part in the program will owe something to her—an odd kind of silent tribute that may persist for a long time.

Introduction

One of the constants in the sequence of human generations, as far back as we have records, is the older ones
bewailing the ignorance of the younger ones. Another
constant is the older ones saying that they know that
all previous older generations bewailed the ignorance
of their younger successors, but that *this time* it really
is uniquely, cataclysmically bad. *Our* younger generation is demonstrating ignorance on a scale that dwarfs
that of all previous ignorant generations; our younger
generation has them all beat when it comes to minds
of desertlike vacuousness. "The kids these days" know
nothing, except the words of pop songs drilled into their
brains through wrecked ears from jabbering iPods. *Our*
younger generation, to a degree like none before it, has
been the victim of years of successful dumbing-down
by TV and Hollywood movies, which have served huge
numbers of them in the place of family life, interactions
with knowledgeable adults, and experience of the natural world.

Those who have taught many years of undergradu-
ate students in universities, where one might expect
better-educated young people to show up, claim that
the ranks of recent years really do take some beating.

"It's not," one professor recently complained to me, "that they don't recall the provisions of the Treaty of Versailles, they don't recall there had been a treaty, or why it occurred, or what a treaty is, or 'Who's Versailles anyway?' and on and on, exposing a seemingly unbounded abyss of ignorance. And they are entirely content in the abyss, concerned in a generally friendly way that I am troubled by their ignorance of pretty well all the history they were taught in school. It isn't, they tell me, relevant to their lives now. And in all their school years clearly no one has shown them how it might be relevant to their lives."

Certainly all those college students had been taught about the Treaty of Versailles in their school years, and a huge number of other things they seem not to know. Dividing fractions, proving that interior opposite angles of a parallelogram are congruent, composing grammatical sentences, analyzing arguments, identifying countries on an unmarked map of the world, and on and on, have been taught to all students, but the knowledge, if it rested in their minds at all, disappeared like frost on a spring morning. Look at the curriculum guides for all those years of school: they are like a vast encyclopedia of human knowledge. But it is as though all that knowledge was taught to students in a foreign language for all the effect it has had on their minds by the time they leave school—according to the results of tests. (These depressing results have been consistent from the influential 1981 Educational Testing Service report [Barrows et al.] and the Nation at Risk report [National Commission on Excellence in Education 1983], to more recent dramatic summaries, such as Bauerlein's charmingly titled *The Dumbest Generation: How the Digital Age Stupefies Young Americans and Jeopardizes Our Future [or, Don't Trust Anyone under 30]* [2008].) A few years on and even the knowledge successfully learned for tests that were triumphantly passed has faded away, slid into the abyss, unattached to anything that can keep it alive in their minds. They are like incontinent amnesiacs at full throttle.

Well, I guess I don't need to labor this—you'll be familiar with the jeremiads. (Who's Jerry?) Easy to moan, but what are we going to do about it? In this book I want to outline a simple proposal, relatively easy to implement, for solving a significant part of the problem. It is, as far as I'm aware, a new idea. If implemented, it just might have a transformative influence on young people's education. The strategy isn't some new method of teaching everything, but rather a proposal for teaching *something* in depth. I'll describe the proposal in chapter 2, after sketching in more detail than I have here the nature of the problem I think this proposal can address.

In the expectation that some hard-hearted readers might have doubts that a simple and relatively easily implemented idea might have a major impact on one of the most intractable problems of schooling, I'll use chapter 3 to examine what seem like the main objections to the proposal, and I will respond to each of the objections. The chapter is designed as a kind of question and answer session, in which a proponent of Learning in Depth is facing members of a school board who are considering the program. Their initial impulse is to reject such an unusual idea out of hand, and this question and answer device enables me to explore the kind of objections people might raise to this proposed program. The fictional school board members are, like most educational administrators, open-minded about new possibilities, but wary, and knowledgeable, about the problems of implementing any new program. This is a long chapter, and it tries to make engaging what is inevitably a rather difficult task of looking in detail at all the things that could go wrong and giving reasons why they can go right. In chapter 4, I'll describe a key feature of the proposal in more detail. In chapter 5, I will offer some principles and practical suggestions for how we might guide students through this new component of the school curriculum. In chapter 6, I will consider in detail another central practical component of the proposal; in chapter 7, I'll suggest steps we can begin to take tomorrow to get this plan underway. This book is intended primarily to describe and propose a novel program that can be built into all schools' curricula, and I will be focusing largely on the practical details of the proposal and how it can be made to work for the educational benefit of students, and teachers, and the school. Some of the readers of the draft manuscript of the book asked for some more theoretical background for the proposal, and so I have written an extensive appendix that will provide a discussion of the foundations of this proposal. Then I'll conclude, and we can all go home.

Books that begin by citing claims that students learn very little in schools may be expected to blame teachers for this failure to deliver the educational goods we expect. But I consider teachers, in general, to be heroic professionals commonly working in enormously difficult conditions, especially when their governments and educational administrators blame them for the schools' apparent inability to "produce" the skills and knowledge desired. I have elsewhere tried to show the real culprits in schools' ineffectiveness (Egan 2002, 2008), and want here to offer a partial solution that will, I hope, appeal to teachers' skills in a somewhat new way and also satisfyingly engage the motives that brought them into the profession in the first place.

Teachers mostly work hard to ensure adequate coverage for the mass of students of the basic knowledge a modern citizen might require. Learning in depth, in as far as this has been pursued in schools, has usually been a kind of educational luxury reserved for high-achieving students. So this proposal might at first seem aimed at the higher set of educational achievers. But that is not the case. This proposal may have a much more beneficial impact on lower achieving students; it may do the most to transform for them the experience of schooling.

The Problem

1

Whether or not our current cohort of students is setting new records in the ignorance stakes, we do have a problem concerning an inadequate return in terms of the knowledge they learn for the high-cost teaching effort expended in schools. What is the point of teaching a curriculum crammed with the wonders of human discoveries and inventions when we see most students come out of our schooling system recalling little of this knowledge and with virtually no sense of its wonder? That is to say, we surely have a problem. And here's a solution that I hope to persuade you is worth trying. As it comes at the problem from a new direction, let me elaborate the problem a little to explain why this unconventional proposal stands a fair chance of resolving it.

Breadth and Depth of Knowledge

Nearly everyone who has tried to describe an image of the educated person, from Plato to the present, includes at least two criteria: first, that educated people must be widely knowledgeable and, second, that they must know *something* in depth. The first criterion is fairly straightforward—pretty well everyone associates being well educated with knowing a fair amount about the world, about its history and geography, about politics in their own and other countries, about what is generally going on in the sciences, about the arts and literature, and so on. That is, a person who really has learned, retained, and somehow made meaningful the curriculum that has been taught in school satisfies the breadth criterion. In addition, we expect that breadth of knowledge not to be some loose assemblage of facts, but also to involve some conceptual schemes that give it order and give the person some general understanding, and we also expect the educated person to have developed habits of critical reflection on what is known, along with a commitment to continuous learning. Such a person is equipped with the knowledge and skills that a modern society requires.

The depth criterion is there because most commentators on education recognize that having a relatively superficial knowledge of many things is somehow not adequate to give an understanding of, to put it a bit vaguely—as it usually is put—the way knowledge works, or the nature of knowledge, or the insecurity of knowledge. By learning something in depth we come to grasp it from the inside, as it were, rather than the way in which we remain always somehow on the outside of that accumulated breadth of knowledge. With regard to the knowledge we learn in breadth, we rely always on the expertise of others; when learning in depth, we develop our own expertise. It is assumed that learning *something* in depth carries over to a better understanding of all our other, "breadth," knowledge.

In everyday classrooms, teachers commonly try to achieve both breadth and depth by covering a topic in a general way and exploring some particular themes in more detail, or by allowing students to choose projects they can pursue in more depth within an overall unit of study. The main curriculum provision schools make for achieving the depth criterion is to enable students in high schools to specialize in something or to develop specialized skills as part of vocational preparation. But in terms of satisfying the depth criterion, these faint moves don't begin to have an impact on the problem. They merely encourage students to learn something a little less superficially.

This proposal is not concerned with the obvious utility value that a lot of specialist knowledge serves for someone working in a technically demanding area or someone in a profession that requires considerable detailed knowledge. Accumulation of relevant "vocational" knowledge cannot achieve what we want educationally, and, anyway, it generally comes far too late in a person's education to achieve what learning in depth can do for the school-aged student.

Breadth Important for All; Depth a Luxury for Some

It is usually assumed, as far as the school system is concerned, that the depth criterion is a bit of a luxury and available mainly to the more academic students or to those in wealthy private schools; the breadth criterion is what we mostly struggle with for the mass of students most of the time ensuring exposure to and coverage of the general information we consider essential for an effective citizen in today's world.

Our currently dominant educational ideas require that we justify curriculum content in terms of its relevance to the kinds of lives students are likely to lead. That criterion leads us to cover a great deal of important knowledge that will have utility in their daily lives. It does not lead to prescribing consistent and deep learning of something that might have no particular relevance to their social lives—indeed it suggests any such prescription would be considered eccentric. That is, we assume that our main task is exposure to a wide breadth of relevant knowledge, and we hope that in among this there will be some topics or subjects in which students' own interests will carry them to greater specialization.

I think there are a number of things wrong with these educational ideas, but here I want to address only the implications for attaining breadth and depth of knowledge. I think we have got it the wrong way round; I think that achieving the depth criterion is a key to also achieving the breadth criterion better. So I will show

how we might manage successful learning in depth, and suggest how this might go some significant way toward solving the more obvious problem of graduates of our school system seeming to know little of the curriculum they have been taught for more than a decade.

Why Depth?

Encouraging students to learn something in depth is not generally seen as essential in our schools, especially when so many students seem to have difficulty mastering even the most basic levels of literacy and numeracy. So, what educational purpose does knowing something in depth serve? Since Plato's days to our own, this question has been posed in terms of what deep knowledge does for the mind. What reasons are usually given? Here are a few:

1. Expertise and Learning How Knowledge Works

The most common claim is a kind of tautology: lacking deep knowledge of *something* is to lack an adequate understanding of what knowledge *is*, and how it functions. If one's knowledge of everything remains at a general and superficial level, one never really comes to appreciate the nature of knowledge. One of the things a person learns in the process of learning in depth is how claims to knowing can be built and attacked and defended—it's all part of the slow process of discovering the insecurity of our claims to know. As noted above, knowing something in depth is like knowing it from the inside, where the student gains expertise, and comes to recognize from one area studied in depth something about how knowledge works in all areas.

People who know nothing in depth—who know everything from the outside—commonly assume that their opinions are the same kind of thing as knowledge. They do not learn adequately the difference between knowledge and their beliefs about things. This leaves them easy prey to those who take advantage of the

gullible—they lack the defenses that deep knowledge can provide. It can also make them assertively confident in their opinions about things where secure knowledge is lacking. During a
few years of teaching in universities I have commonly noted a
strong positive correlation between students who have difficulty
stringing a grammatical sentence together or making a marginally
coherent argument and confidence in their opinions about how to
organize societies, run the country's foreign policy, and instruct
others how to live.

It's not that people who lack deep knowledge come to believe
nothing, but rather that they will believe anything. (Alien abduc-
tions; monsters of all kinds—especially the unhygienic undead;
vampires and supernatural events—without which many movies
would not get off the ground; fantastic conspiracy theories; pos-
session by exotic spirits; access to memories from a previous life;
a stunning array of crazy "urban myths"; and so, bizarrely, on.)
Learning about something in depth can provide some inocula-
tion against confusing opinion or wild claim with knowledge, and
one of the products of learning in depth is gaining greater delight
from learning about the wonders of the natural world than from
tacky, clichéd, superficial falsehoods.

Incorporating some of the ideas supporting learning in depth,
Howard Gardner gives a more focused, precise, and compelling
set of arguments for why learning in depth is crucial to producing
an adequately educated person and an adequate understanding of
any topic. He shows, taking particular examples, that only by disciplined work can one get below the parochial level of knowledge
that is too common. Furthermore, he shows that in-depth knowledge can bring about a state of mind such that students "will have
a sense of what it means—of how it feels—to understand consequential topics" (1999, p. 245). He notes, too, that such understanding gained from the study of one topic or issue gives one
a sense of the nature of knowledge and what it means to properly understand something that serves as a "litmus test" to apply
to other topics and issues. He argues that currently our schools

are less effective than they need be because they try to teach too much too superficially; they would be much more successful by focusing on a smaller number of consequential topics and ensuring students learn them in depth.

2. The Pleasure of Learning

Educational philosophers have consistently argued that the educated person needs to combine both breadth of knowledge about the world and depth of knowledge about something in particular. Plato, in the *Republic*, most conspicuously argued for the importance of learning in depth. His curriculum for the best educated was to take fifty years of study. More recently, Peters and Hirst (1970) have also emphasized that only by learning something in depth can a person escape from the confusions that commonly accompany a superficial knowledge base, and that this achievement yields something we consider worthwhile for its own sake, and so call pleasurable.

There is a related aesthetic benefit connected with knowing something in depth. Without this pleasure, the idea of learning for its own sake can never really take hold. The alternatives are always utilitarian learning—justified by some specific use to which it will be put—and entertainment. This would seem to describe the norm for most people; we learn what we need to know for some purpose, and then we turn to entertainment to fill our time. The related problem is that nearly all learning in schools is coerced in some way—no teaching without evaluation or assessment of some kind. It's as though we assume students will learn only if they know "it will be on the test later." The very structure of schooling today seems to militate against students developing the accumulating pleasure of learning for its own sake.

Knowing nothing much in significant depth also means that the victim's understanding never becomes clear. The problem here is not that a person well equipped with a wide range of knowledge can't lead a perfectly contented life, but rather that a very peculiar human pleasure is denied them. That pleasure comes from the particular wisdom available only after one recognizes the nature of the knowledge one holds. Once one knows something in depth, the resulting understanding spreads to everything; without some deep knowledge, it spreads to nothing much.

3. Stimulating the Imagination

A less obvious benefit of learning in depth concerns its importance in the stimulation and development of students' imaginations. Being able to find particular knowledge in the mountains of information in libraries or on the Internet can be educationally valuable, of course. The downside of the emphasis on such procedural skills, however, is a disastrous underestimation of the importance of actually *knowing* things and having access to knowledge in memory—because the imagination works only with what we know. That is, the more we know about something, the more imaginative we can be about it (Egan 1997). Knowing a lot doesn't mean we *will* be imaginative, of course, but we *cannot* be imaginative about what we don't know. At the end of their schooling, students who have been through a Learning in Depth program will have immensely stimulating material that can engage and enrich their imaginations when it comes to thinking about their topics and things related to them. The imagination is not some idle spinning of airy nothings, as it has sometimes been represented, but is one of the great workhorses of learning (Egan 2008). Without serious and significant knowledge, the imagination cannot do its best work. Ignorance impoverishes the imagination because ignorance leaves one with little to work with. Also the more we know about something, the more imaginatively we can solve problems related to it. Richness of knowledge is what gets imaginations up in the morning.

4. Projects and Their Focus

The persistence of Kilpatrick's "Project Method" in Western education systems also speaks to the recognition by many that greater depth in learning has obvious benefits. Kilpatrick believed that properly organized projects involved students not simply in learning a topic in greater depth but also as a part of purposeful social activity, such that learning enriched the students' experience and their understanding of moral and democratic life. Recognition of the values of more engaged and systematic learning that a well-organized project allows has ensured the continuation of this form of teaching today. Among its most energetic promoters are Lilian Katz and Sylvia Chard (1989). They suggest that projects offer a complementary form of teaching to regular forms of systematic instruction, especially in the early school years. It is a form of teaching they, and many others, believe has some clear and potent advantages over regular modes of instruction.

The Learning in Depth program shares with the Project Method a recognition of the values students derive from learning something in greater detail and developing a fuller understanding than is common with much of the curriculum. But LiD is also different in a number of important ways, in particular in its assumptions about how much individual work the student has to do before gaining really significant insights into any topic.

5. Deep Learning and the Sense of Self

Another educational benefit that is sometimes identified comes to fruition when the understanding that can result from learning in depth interacts with our sense of self. I don't want to make this into a kind of spiritual discussion, but many do use that kind of language to describe how deep knowledge can give us insights into ourselves, into our human condition. It is as a result of learning something in depth that we can connect with the layer of human understanding that leads to what we often vaguely call wisdom. Not just any kind of depth learning will produce these benefits of course, so it will be necessary in designing our LiD programs that we put in place criteria for the kinds of topics that can stimulate this deeper kind of understanding.

6. Learning in Depth and Humility

One of the great paradoxes of education is that only when one knows something deeply can one recognize how little one actually knows, that the more one learns the more one realizes there is to learn about any topic. Superficial knowledge is a curse of education—the target of Pope's "a little learning is a dangerous thing."

When people learn something superficially they often easily assume they know everything about the topic. One hears people with only the most marginal information confidently claiming certainty about things of which they know very little. As one acquires more and more knowledge about something, and as one begins to amass genuine expertise, one learns something about how insecure our knowledge really is and also how little we truly understand about almost anything. This is a sobering experience, and sobriety of this kind is one of the gifts of learning in depth. Realizing how little one knows is not disabling and is unlikely to cause depression and result in lack of interest in the topic; instead, it is properly exhilarating, giving a thrilling sense of bringing knowledge into our minds in ways that recognize both what we know and what remains to be known, and perhaps also gives a sense of the mystery of knowledge too—adding a dimension to the engagement of imagination. This sense of how little we know even about what we know best generates an important sense of humility before the world of knowledge, and adds to our sense of who we are and what we can hope to achieve.

7. Oral and Literate Cultures' Knowledge

Some of the above claims about why it is important to learn something in depth are maybe not entirely compelling, if only because the language in which they tend to be couched is a little vague. It is vague in part because understanding the meaning of some of the claims requires us to have achieved the experience described.

If we haven't, then there remains a sense of discomfort and imprecision about the meaning of some of the claims, and we can only extrapolate from experiences we have had in the direction of more in-depth learning than any of us has likely achieved. We tend to be willing to give some of these claims *some* credence because they do describe experiences we at least partly recognize. And we are inclined to accept some claims because they have been made by people whose great expertise we admire. Pope's "a little learning is a dangerous thing" resonates because we have all seen some buffoon making overconfident assertions based on superficial knowledge. And we might recognize the way in which something we have studied in depth opens up new dimensions of understanding for us, and this stimulates a curious kind of exhilaration and also humility in the face of what remains to be learned. And maybe we can recognize from our own experience that we can be more imaginative about what we know most than we can be about things with which we are less familiar.

But still, these claims are all somewhat impressionistic, even though one or more of them might ring true for us. What I want to discuss now is something that is more profound and complex. For the past couple of hundred years, during which anthropologists have made contact with oral cultures with the intention of studying what used to be called "primitive" people, some puzzles have arisen. The reason we no longer talk about "primitive" people is due to the slow and somewhat painful discovery that people in oral cultures, who initially seemed to anthropologists and people in Western societies generally to be incapable of reasoning, were in fact no less sophisticated in their thinking than the anthropologists studying them. Some of the insights that have led to our better understanding the thinking of people in oral cultures are due to a number of anthropologists, among whom it seems appropriate to mention Claude Lévi-Strauss, who died in the week I am writing this and whose book *The Savage Mind* (1966) played an important role in exposing something about the logic of oral cultural thinking. Also influential in this regard was

Harold Conklin's (1955) Yale Ph.D. thesis, which studied a tribe of forest-dwelling people in the Philippines. Conklin showed that the knowledge of plants of the average person in those forest environments was vastly superior to that of almost anyone in Europe or the United States, and also that their classificatory systems had much in common with the most sophisticated taxonomies in modern biology.

The relevance of this for the Learning in Depth project becomes clearer when we discover, with relatively recent anthropologists, that almost anyone in these oral cultures, when asked to name as many trees as they can, will list literally hundreds of trees. Not only can they name what seems to us an almost impossible number of trees, but they have a huge amount of knowledge about their conditions of growth, the possible uses of their various woods, their ecological relationships with other plants and animals, and so on. This seems to us astonishing in part because we can't manage anything like this, yet such knowledge is commonplace in oral cultures. When modern university students in the United States are asked to name all the trees they know, they may on average eek out five or six names: "Oak, pine, spruce, . . . cherry . . . (giggle) evergreen, . . . Christmas tree, is that a kind of tree? . . . So what do kids say, big tree, small tree?" (Atran and Medin 2009, p. 2.). This leads to the paradox reported by many anthropologists "that with greater formal education comes lesser knowledge" (Atran and Medin 2009, p. 2).

Well, yes, we might respond uncomfortably and defensively about our relative ignorance, but people in oral cultures don't know anything about the details of computer technology and the endless uses to which one can put the applications of an iPhone. Their extensive knowledge of trees is just a function of what occupies their attention. Such a response does acknowledge the intricacy and complexity of thinking in oral cultures, at least, but is it really satisfactory? Might we still consider our almost total lack of knowledge about the natural world around us, relative to that of members of oral cultures, a problem for us? Have we lost something important with our gain of literacy and modern technologies? Maybe our real problem is less that we lack this knowledge than that we think we don't need it?

Atran and Medin argue extensively that our modern loss of knowledge about the natural world affects the way we behave toward it. Their concern is the cognitive consequences of this lack of natural world knowledge, and they clearly think that even the intense knowledge of some aspects of technology that a few people master is no substitute for the cognitive losses that result from our near-total ignorance of nature. People who know so little, when faced with thinking about the natural world, have hardly any reliable resources to think *with* and can thus use only the blandest reasoning strategies at their disposal, which are utterly inadequate to the task at hand. And, drawing on one of the earlier points above, such people—we/us!—find imaginative engagement almost impossible, except again in the most bland, and largely sentimental, way. Nothing is an adequate substitute for deep knowledge.

Elsewhere I have discussed both what we gain and what we have lost with literacy and its accompanying forms of thought (Egan 1988, 1990). The cognitive strategies that have to be deployed in oral cultures to remember things involve a set of techniques that include framing information in story structures (myths), using rhyme and rhythm, evoking vivid images in the mind, deploying rich metaphors, and elaborating logical structures from binary oppositions—in short using a set of techniques that tie emotions and imaginations vividly in with the material to be learned. Much of my educational work with young children and their teachers has been based on trying to show how we too can deploy these techniques in planning and teaching so that children's emotions and imaginations can be caught up in the material of the curriculum, enabling them to learn more effectively. But none of these techniques can come into play if children are not accumulating the knowledge that adequate deployment of these basic techniques of meaning-making requires.

It's not that these techniques are simply utilitarian and appropriate in oral cultures while other techniques are appropriate for our literate culture, so we can happily ignore this apparent loss that has come with the immense gains of literacy and its reasoning strategies. The cognitive strategy we see in the flexible deployment of metaphors, for example, is not merely of use only in the oral cultures that brought it to a high pitch of refinement; it is of value to anyone today who wants flexibility and creativity in their thinking.

These sets of strategies, both oral cultural and literate, serve us like cognitive tool kits that enrich our ability to make sense of the world and of our experience. The richer our set of strategies, the richer sense we make of the world and our own experience within it. So we would be wise to try to preserve as many of the techniques developed in our cultural history as possible—especially as it is clear that some of those later developed literacy induced techniques rely on some the earlier oral cultural techniques to work adequately. The story structuring of oral cultures is a foundation for our endless modern uses of narrative—when you turn on the TV evening news you see one story after another, and listen to reporters who have honed the skill to describe actual events in a manner that brings out as vividly as possible their emotional meaning. Also it is hard to argue for ignorance when discussing education, as is the position of those who might be inclined to think that we need not worry about what we have patently lost in the massive decline of knowledge about the natural world.

How these techniques of enriching the meaning of what is to be learned can come into play while children begin learning in depth will be dealt with later in this book. For now I just want to add the observation about our catastrophic ignorance of the natural world, and its cognitive consequences, as another reason to consider the educational value of LiD. Especially if we choose our topics from the natural world, we can enable every student to build up both a quantity and a richly meaningful intensity of knowledge, which might go some way toward saving us from our current inability to think well about the natural world and our place within it.

Depth of Knowledge for All

Lacking depth of knowledge, then, contributes to superficiality and inadequate understanding of the meaning even of the knowledge one has, makes one gullible and credulous, deprives one of the pleasures of learning for its own sake, impoverishes the imagination, and leaves us incompetent to think sensibly about the natural world of which we are a part. Quite a rap sheet!

While it isn't as easy to pinpoint the value of learning in depth as it is to point to the value of learning purely utilitarian knowledge, there are reasons to accept that learning in depth is educationally important for all students. And the reasons for learning in depth do go to the heart of a crucial aspect of education. The paradoxical element in all this—which should make it attractive to the educational system's paymasters—is that learning in depth in a nonutilitarian way is what really can make utilitarian learning effective. Our current focus on superficial "breadth" knowledge, after all, is hardly delivering the educational goods. A close look at a proposal for ensuring depth for all makes sense.

I should also mention the intuitive appeal of learning something in depth. Whenever I have spoken with teachers about this idea during the past year or so nearly always someone says that they recall with the most pleasure something they had to study in detail. As one teacher a few weeks ago said: "In grade 8 I did a year long special study on pyramids. I ate, drank, and slept with pyramids in my mind! It was my happiest memory of school, and I remember so much of it vividly today."

In this chapter I have looked at a number of arguments given to support the general idea of learning in depth. The programs associated with some of these arguments are quite different from one other, and they are all unlike the proposal I will make. My aim here has not been to indicate agreement with all these ideas so much as to indicate that many educators over many years have recognized important educational values that result from knowing something in depth. Despite this long recognition, we have not been obviously successful in achieving what these arguments and programs have described as their aim.

The Proposal

How might students gain such depth of knowledge? Well, this proposal can be stated very simply: The basic idea is that children will be randomly assigned, during the first week of schooling, a particular topic to learn about through their whole school career, in addition to the usual curriculum. Topics might include such things as *apples, the wheel, mollusks, railways, leaves, ships, cats, spices,* etc. Students will meet regularly with their supervising teachers, who will give guidance, suggestions, and help as students build personal portfolios on their topics. The aim is that students, by the end of their schooling, will have built genuine expertise. The expectation is that this process will transform their relationship to and understanding of the nature of knowledge. It should also transform for each child the experience of schooling. It should also be emotionally satisfying, in the way that unforced learning commonly is.

By the time they graduate from school the students will be immensely knowledgeable about *something*. Indeed, each student will know close to as much about some specific topic as most experts. They will also recognize that the topic about which they have such expertise is something that has expanded so vastly in their understanding that they realize they know little compared to what there is to know about it.

The fruits of this curriculum innovation will be students who know something in great depth, and also who know something about the nature of knowledge, and who will have developed some humility and expertise in the face of casual knowledge claims by the inadequately educated. You might, skeptically, think that it might rather lead to students revolting against their topic, which becomes increasingly distasteful to them, or that it will lead them to intense boredom, or that they should, at least, be given choice in the topic, and the freedom to change their focus whenever they get fed up with a particular topic. And you may think, anyway, it would be impossible to implement. Mind you, one image the above proposal might bring to mind is of little Nathan howling in misery because he has just been told he has to study *dust* for the next twelve years, whereas his friend Jane has got *the circus*. Later I will discuss how one can make the reception of their topics into an important ceremony, in which there will be considerable anticipation and excitement about discovering what each student's topic is to be, and how we can mitigate problems such as Nathan's potential misery on discovering his topic. The students, and the rest of us, need to recognize that an underlying principle of this proposal is that everything is wonderful, if only we learn enough about it. Well, maybe not everything is wonderful, but it is ignorance that leads to boredom and failure to engage with topics. Bear with me on this one, and we'll come back to such problems.

Sara, let us imagine, was assigned the topic of apples in her first week of school. She began her portfolio by drawing red and green apples, and indicated that one was a McIntosh and the other a Granny Smith. Then there was a list of apple varieties. The first part of the list was composed from the varieties Sara had found in shops, and then she had added some extra ones that grew locally that she found at a farmer's market her parents took her to. Then there was a more elaborate list, clearly pulled from the Internet, but she had made some additional notes next to those she had eaten—notes about size and color and taste. She had a five-star system to indicate which she thought best.

Later Sara had noted that her list included only a very few of the 7,500 varieties that currently are cultivated around the world. She began a file on apple history, which included pieces about the earliest sweet and flavorful apples, such as those we eat today, being first identified in Kazakhstan four thousand years ago. She had a map identifying the area, and also a world map with small notes indicating places where there were very old records that mention apples.

Then she had a file on stories about apples: the Bible story of the Garden of Eden—though it mentions only "fruit," it is usually assumed to indicate an apple; the Swiss story of William Tell shooting the apple off his son's head; John Chapman, better known as "Johnny Appleseed"; the story of Newton's falling apple; and so on. Then she had a file made up of games and verses and sayings about apples, and it included a section in which she had written definitions of such phrases as "the apple of my eye," or "one rotten apple spoils the whole barrel," and why people say, "An apple a day keeps the doctor away." She has a picture of an old pirate ship under sail, with a brimming barrel of red apples on board, which she knows are there because they will save the sailors from scurvy, and will do the same for us.

As you flick through her portfolio as she enters secondary school you will see segments on the fact that apple trees are part of the rose family and that the biggest apple was approximately four pounds. She has a small file explaining why apples float. There is a note that the current Lady apple was first cultivated by an Etruscan woman called Api, and in France it is still called "pomme d'Api"—a good way to be remembered, Sara noted. The Greeks and Romans prized apples, and had cultivated about twenty varieties: Sara has a complex "family tree" showing the development from those early apples to our current abundance of varieties.

She also has a few pages of description of the Trojan War, with pictures of Helen and Achilles and all their storied crew. This excursion into the mists of myth becoming history grew out of her discovery of stories about apples, and one in particular about Eris, who, excluded from a wedding, tossed a golden apple that was to be awarded to the most beautiful woman present. Paris of Troy was appointed judge, and he, fatefully, chose the goddess Aphrodite after she tempted him with the most beautiful woman in the world, Helen of Sparta. His taking Helen with him back to Troy launched the thousand ships and brought down the topless towers, and caused the death of noble Hector, tamer of horses, and the great Achilles, and the wandering and final return to Ithaca of wily Ulysses. All these adventures spun out of an apple.

In Sara's portfolio is a beautiful large sheet on which she had written, almost like a medieval manuscript, a copy of W. B. Yeats's poem "The Song of Wandering Aengus," with illustrations of the "glimmering girl / With apple blossom in her hair" and of Wandering Aengus who had looked for the glimmering girl for so long, and thinking when he had found her that they would pluck "till time and times were done / the silver apples of the moon, the golden apples of the sun."

She had a page attached, in which she noted that she first didn't understand it well, but was attracted by its magic, and now she knows it so well, it goes everywhere with her, as do many other songs and poems and texts about apples, each able to generate rich images at appropriate times, and each making her life that little bit more interesting. Yeats's poem added a dimension to her sense of apples. It set up resonances that will stay with her for the rest of her life.

Well, perhaps "Yeah, right!" is the appropriate response to this scenario. It is rather idealistic, of course. My aim here has not been to try to describe how the program might look year by year or what its practical problems might be—that's something for the rest of the book—but to give a quick sense of where it can take a student, idealistic or not. It is intended to introduce students not just to a mass of detailed information about a topic, but also to enable them to discover ramifying knowledge and understanding about human experience, and to engage their imaginations and emotions. Not every topic can do that, so we will have to spend some time working out what range of specific topics will serve this project adequately, as well as looking at some new forms of teaching that such a project might call on. We will also have to examine in more practical detail what these portfolios might look like, where they might be stored, what students' presentations might be like and what purposes they perform, and a number of other matters that will bring the ideal into the realm of the everyday school and its routines.

That's it—a simple concept with wide-ranging ramifications: a new element of schooling that need not take very much time from the regular curriculum, but which will likely have a profound impact on the students, their knowledge, and their approach to the rest of the curriculum as the years go by. If implemented, students would all begin a new educational process of *really* learning something in depth. They would slowly work on accumulating their portfolios, and learning more and more. The quality of their learning would change with time, and their own interests would influence the direction of their portfolios. All the school system would require is that the portfolio keeps growing and the students keep learning more about their special topic.

Initially students will likely need significant help from the teacher charged to guide development of their portfolios. But as time goes by, students' knowledge of their topic will exceed that of the teacher, and they will become increasingly autonomous in the way they continue their studies—some students might obviously be expected to become more independent earlier in their studies than others. Teachers will continue to monitor the portfolio's development, and can counsel students and respond to their questions about new dimensions of their topic that they might explore.

As I suggested earlier, we should differentiate this new feature of the curriculum from the regular work students do in their classes. The introduction of the topics to students, though arbitrarily assigned, should be marked as important, as the beginning of what will be an unusual lifelong relationship. I think it

important that the assignment of topics be made in some ceremonial context.

It could be something as simple as a kind of graduation ceremony, in which the students would be given an initial portfolio
folder. It would seem desirable also that in some part of the ceremony, perhaps early on, the student performs an act, a taking
on of the topic, and that there should be some symbolic expression whereby the student publicly claims ownership of the topic.
Perhaps, the student should be the first one to voice the topic in
public, with help if necessary. This need not be stressful for the
students, and they may be supported in all parts of the ceremony,
but they themselves will be the ones to announce in public what
their topic is. The initial portfolio container they are given might
have in it, for example, a tile that the student might then place on
a special wall in the school on which multicolored tiles create an
attractive mosaic.

The purpose of the ceremony is to emphasize the importance
of what the students are taking on and also to engage the students' commitment to their special topic. It might be good to
hold the ceremony on a weekend morning, or at some time at
which as many parents as possible can attend. I think also that
the ceremony should be serious, and, crucially, lack any element
of patronization. Children are no less intelligent than adults; they
simply have had less experience and know less. This ceremony
marks an initiation into the great human adventure of coming to
know the world in symbolic terms.

A further distinctive feature of this project is that students will
work alone for much of the time. They will meet with their supervising teacher, with older students who may have be working
on the same topic, with parent volunteers, with college student
volunteers, with school teacher-librarians, and with their friends.
But the topic is theirs; it will be pursued in directions they wish;
it is not to be graded or become in any way a part of credentialing or competition for awards or college or university places; it is
an exploration of some area of knowledge that may initially seem
uncomplicated but will gradually come to be seen as infinite.

I should emphasize a couple of features of the LiD program, even though it seems that mentioning them has little impact on some people's assumptions about how it will work. First, the student's topic is not intended to replace the rest of the curriculum! That is, the LiD program is a simple add-on to the current curriculum. Students continue with their regular schooling exactly as they do today, but LiD is an added program. We will have to explore the practical problems this raises later, but here I just want to emphasize that students are not supposed to learn everything "through" their topic. (The confusion may be due to some past proposals recommending precisely this replacement of the usual curriculum. Some radical theorists have suggested that students should begin with some self-chosen focus or questions. The curriculum would then be composed from the inquiries students use in trying to answer these important questions. Supporters of such a proposal expect, or hope, that as students follow up their interests they will gradually discover the whole world of knowledge driven by their own interests [e.g., Postman and Weingartner 1971]. LiD takes a quite different approach.)

Second, LiD is not to be another class. I don't envision anything like a teaching slot given over to everyone working in a classroom on their LiD projects. Again, we will explore what organizational problems such an innovation might create, but LiD is not some alternative pedagogy that is supposed to replace current forms.

Objections and Responses ## 3

Let's assume we have a group of school administrators who have just heard the LiD proposal, and have been asked to consider introducing it into their school district. Their initial impulse is to reject such an eccentric and novel idea out of hand. After all, if it were likely to have the educational benefits claimed, someone would have suggested it before, and it would have been put into practice somewhere, wouldn't it? They are, like most educational administrators, open-minded about new possibilities, but wary, and knowledgeable, about the problems of implementing any new program. And, being human, they tend to look for reasons not to do something extra, especially if it looks as though it could involve a mess of problems, and might possibly antagonize some teachers, administrators, or, worse, parents.

Here is a set of the objections our administrators might make to the proposal. Let's assume we are going round the table to see what problems they foresee. Some are more skeptical than others, but all of them represent aspects of the dominant ideas that currently drive our schools. The fictional objectors will be given some sketchy background, to indicate the possible sources of the objections they make. In addition, let us assume that the responses are being delivered by a proponent of the LiD program who is in the hot seat before the committee of administrators. (The illusion of interacting with the committee will be interrupted occasionally by my indicating points later in the book where some issues will be developed further—rather than trying to include the whole book in this "discussion." I'll also use this as an opportunity to fill out some details about how the program might work in more detail.)

One of the peculiarities of this exercise, given that I am advocating implementation of the LiD program, is that it is much easier, and more fun, writing the critical attacks on the program than defending it. Perhaps if my advocacy is successful here and there, it will be possible in the future to show examples of what currently has to rely on projections of possibilities based on arguments, reasons, and surmises.

Objection 1. Students will soon become bored with their topics.

A newly appointed superintendent of schools. She taught in three different elementary schools for fifteen years before becoming vice-principal and then principal of a large urban school. She has an M.Ed., in which she wrote a special project on children's intellectual development, and also an Ed.D. specializing in curriculum leadership.

Even if you might manage to get a typical five-year-old to take on studying *leaves*, or those other topics you suggest, there just isn't the interest to keep a child pursuing the one topic like that for a dozen years. Children have a short attention span at the age you want to begin this depth study. They will not be able to focus attention onto a single topic in the way you require. There's only so much interest value in *trees* or *apples* for a child at age five or six, and it isn't much! So they will easily get bored, especially when they have so little support from the supervising teacher. After a month the average child will have forgotten what the topic is they are supposed to be studying.

Even constant teacher help wouldn't stop children from easily becoming bored. You might have in your mind some bright, middle-class child who could be persuaded to go for this with parents' constant support. But most kids won't have that home support—how much does the average parent know about *trees* or *apples?* They could tell their child everything they know in half an hour at the most. And very few parents will be interested in finding out more and more about *leaves* or *birds* to be able to keep helping their child. If they have three children, each with a different topic, the whole scenario, even in the ideal situation, becomes impossible.

So where is the child supposed to turn? They can't read very well in the early years of their participation in this scheme, and won't be able to tour the Internet for information. The whole thing ignores what the average child brings to learning. This project assumes little scientists eager to learn. That's not the reality of most children in most schools that I have been dealing with for more than a couple of decades. I'm afraid this is more fantasy than reality; it just ignores the way average students' minds work; it assumes there will be growing interest where, for most kids, there will just be growing boredom. And worse it ignores the large number of children who suffer from learning disabilities of one kind or another. Our district has a high number of special needs students, and I can't see this being of any use to them at all. They wouldn't be able to get started.

What are even the average students supposed to be finding out about *trees,* year in and year out? I know biologists can specialize and do research for years, but these children will not be able to run their own experiments, which these days need expensive equipment and laboratories. The students I have known over the years have their enthusiasms—and it's no secret what they are. Accumulating knowledge about *the wheel* or *apples* or even *the circus* is no part of what captures young people's minds these days. Maybe it might have worked in elite schools a hundred years ago, but today's reality is very different.

I'm sorry to be so negative. But I'm not convinced that the solution to our educational problems—and I am the first to admit we have problems—is a weird innovation like this. We have drugs, family crises, easy access to all kinds of worrying entertainment on the Internet and other media, and a ton of other problems. Kids studying *apples* for a dozen years just doesn't make it onto my radar as worth spending any time and money on.

Response to: Students will soon become bored with their topics.

The superintendent makes a number of good points, and I'm not sure I will be able to answer them all to her satisfaction. But let's start, as she does, with the observation that children will quickly get bored with their topic because at the beginning stages of this scheme the average child has a very short attention span. I'll introduce my response with a brief anecdote. A number of years ago I was asked to take part in a radio talk show with a couple of other educators, one a teacher, the other a professor of child psychology. The topic was children's attention span, and how it was being made shorter and shorter by typical TV shows and the kinds of electronic entertainments available for kids today. The interviewer set the tone by regretfully taking it for granted that children increasingly couldn't attend to anything for any length of time. Some studies were cited—the actual stimulus for the show—and then the "experts" were asked to give their views. I felt it useful to point out that the interviewer could have reported on the studies and then could have given the responses that we were being called on to give, without any need to have gone to all the trouble of bringing all of us together in the studio. Instead, we had an interviewer and three other people, and if we weren't off the air in eight minutes, for the ads, then we would get the hook or the slow fade into silence. We would be able to talk only for a very few minutes in total, and the interviewer was energetically trying to focus on areas where we might disagree. That is, the format of the show was taking for granted in its adult listeners exactly the condition it was supposed to be regretting in children.

In my experience, children's attention span, like typical adults', is greatly stretchable depending on what engages it. If the worry is that children's attention span is very brief in classrooms, then that would seem to me to suggest what is happening in the classroom isn't very interesting. In some classrooms children show remarkable attention spans, and in others there is hardly any attention at all.

I don't want to suggest that's all that needs to be said about it; children clearly do vary in the attention they give to any topic. But I don't think children are significantly different from adults in this. That is, whatever other objections might be made to this proposal, the fact that children are supposed to have short attention spans isn't one I can take seriously.

More serious is the point the superintendent connects with it—that their attention-span deficit, or some other cause, will mean that they will quickly become bored with the topic given to them. In the end, this is an objection that won't be resolved by assertion, but by experience. But, first, we need to have good reasons even to try a pilot project. The good reason is that much experience suggests that exactly the opposite is true.

All my experience of education suggests that boredom is a symptom of inadequate knowledge or ignorance. The more you know about something, the more interesting it becomes. ("Everything is wonderful" is, again, one of the overstated underlying slogans that have been attached to this LiD proposal.) The person without the intellectual resources deep knowledge can provide is much more likely to be bored.

Well, that's a response that is maybe adequate for perhaps the third and subsequent years of this project, but initially, at least, students' knowledge, I have to agree, will not be in "depth"; they have to start learning about their topic as they would any other subject in school. In part that initial engagement can be encouraged by the ceremonial treatment given to the students' reception of their topics, which I'll discuss in chapter 6, and in part it can be encouraged by the principles for engaging their imaginations in topics that I'll discuss in chapter 5. Quite quickly, even in the first year, the student will likely know more about their topic than they will know about anything else they have been taught. So the point about boredom being a product of ignorance is one that should give us some confidence that students will likely become less bored by their topics early on. In fact, to the surprise even of the teachers involved, reports on the first pilot projects that are, as I write, into their second year, indicate children already are strongly attached to "their" topics and are eager to continue with them.

The superintendent's point about the inadequacy of supervising teachers having only monthly meetings with students early in the process seems to me telling. We need to plan for weekly meetings, or perhaps even more, at this stage, even if they are quite short, or consider some further support system to get this off the ground. I'm sure some member of the board will make the objection that this project won't work because it requires unacceptable time, energy, money, and other resources, so perhaps I can leave discussing this, and parental involvement, until I respond to such objections later.

I think that learning in depth is not something that is suitable only for bright middle-class students who will have plenty of parental support. Indeed, I think it offers more to those students for whom current schooling offers so little. At present, low-achieving students, who may have no home support for learning, get hardly any nourishment of the kind that schools promise to offer to all children. Remember that "equality of opportunity" promised to all children, and all those optimistic "mission statements" plastered on a hundred thousand school walls and Web sites?

What this scheme offers is something from which all children can get some intellectual nourishment. It is, indeed, based on the belief, which you might reject, that learning about the world around us is intrinsically interesting to everyone. The more we know, the more interesting it becomes. It is boring only to the ignorant. That's just how our minds are. This project is an attempt to strike at the heart of ignorance.

I agree that students beginning to develop their portfolios will not be doing experiments like scientists. But I can't see why they can't do their own small experiments, and experiments of different kinds that do not require a biologist. Or perhaps they could find a biologist to help them do some experiments with *leaves* that will show something of their nature. If this innovation becomes routine in schools, we might begin to see ways in which children can be put in touch with experts for some of their tuition as time goes by. Maybe, if the student is given the topic of *the solar system,* a meeting can be arranged with an astronomer. All topics will have experts in the outside world, and we might begin to see procedures attracting such people to work, even if only for small amounts of time, with children who are becoming experts in particular topics. Certainly one might see university professors counting such involvement with schools as part of their "service" expectation.

I think the assumption that there will be reluctance to learn, and boredom from learning, just one thing in increasing depth year after year is based on some of our experience with schools as they currently exist today. For all kinds of reasons that many educators have discussed over the last century the early years curriculum has been systematically stripped of challenging intellectual activity. It isn't the intellectually challenging topics that bore children, it's the vacuousness of so much of the early school curriculum that leaves them gasping for intellectual air. Under the influence of odd ideas such as that children are "concrete" thinkers, we have removed almost anything of interest and complexity. There is also the strange belief that young children's minds are tied to the local and immediate (while they are fascinated by dinosaurs, wicked witches, and star warriors!). Well, we'll come back to this issue soon.

The common boredom and children's lack of energy to learn is not due to the fact that they behave that way in the face of challenging topics, but rather that's what the current superficial curriculum does to them. I am prescribing a cure to the problem that this objection raises as a reason the cure won't work—if you can untangle that. I mean, this proposal intends to overcome the boredom with curriculum topics that the superintendent sees as a reason it won't work.

She is also concentrating almost entirely on the earliest phase of the scheme—which is obviously sensible as she thinks the whole thing can't get underway for the reasons she gives. But try to imagine what it might be like after twenty or thirty years in operation in a school system, when it's taken for granted as a feature of everyone's education. Children will start school and be prepared by friends and families for the big event of finding out their topic. My expectation is that such topics will be greeted as friends, because that is what they will have become for everyone who will have learned something in genuine depth. And it will be a friend that will be reliably with them for years, and, in some profound sense, for life. Through all the changes of grades and teachers and schools, they will have one constant and growing topic that will provide a stable intellectual anchor for their whole school career.

Objection 2. The arbitrariness is absurd. Student choice is
   important to such a scheme.
A physical education teacher for twenty-three years before being elected to the school board, he has special responsibility as the representative to the city's Advisory Council with regard to Children and Youth. He has an M.Ed. degree in physical education.

I don't think the proposal is as hopeless as my colleague suggests, but I do think that students should be given some choice. You could spend the first half year or so working with the children to see where their interests lie. Let them take on a few topics and see which ones they get a spark from.

   Just assigning students topics is unimaginative and won't do much for their imaginations. Think of the kid in the first week of school: Joe, you will spend twelve years studying *mothballs*. Boom. That's it. Why is there no choice? If you are going to push this scheme, you might get some people to consider it if students were allowed to choose a topic that connects with their own interests. Also they should be given the chance to change their topic if they lose interest in it, allowing them to try a new topic that they think will be more engaging. So I'd be willing to give it a shot as long as there is much more flexibility built into it.

At least you could say that the kids will study one topic to grade 8, but then they would have a choice to go on with their topic or change to something else that they can choose at this time.

I remember my own years in school. I was one of those kids who got enthusiasms about something, and I used to annoy some of my teachers asking for more information about castles, or whatever. But these enthusiasms didn't last for very long. I did have the usual enthusiasm for dinosaurs when I was a kid, and then I remember the castle thing really got me from, I'd say, about eight to twelve—I used to build castles out of Lego, I'd be drawing them all the time, and when we visited Europe I drove my parents nuts wanting to visit every castle in the place. I think this was all good, and the changing nature of what we are interested in should be accommodated by this scheme. So, I'd push for more choice, more flexibility, and an easy ability to change topics.

I'm interested that the topics you mentioned in your proposal were all fairly academic in orientation, mostly science-oriented, natural world items. There was nothing in physical education, nor much in the arts, nor in a number of other areas. I think you'll need to give a much clearer account of what can serve as appropriate learning-in-depth topics before I'd be happy to sign on to this innovation.

Response to: The arbitrariness is absurd. Student choice is important to such a scheme.

In the 1950s there was a study, which unfortunately I can no longer locate, of the range of children's interests between countries that had multiple TV channels and those that had only one. It was found, contrary to expectations, that in countries with multiple channels children's range of interests was significantly narrower. It makes intuitive sense, of course. Given a choice we go to what is comfortable and familiar. One aim of education is to enlarge students' interests. We won't achieve that by allowing them constantly to choose what they are familiar with. Quite the opposite, as the TV study showed. There are good enough reasons to preserve the arbitrariness, though there may be cases where a change might be allowed.

We usually grow to find interesting whatever we learn about in depth—unless we are learning only for utilitarian reasons or against our will. (The old saying in monasteries was that his cell becomes irksome to the monk who constantly finds excuses to leave it, but the monk who keeps to his cell grows to love it.) The underlying principle that guides the arbitrariness is that *everything* is interesting; and the more you know, the more the imagination can play with knowledge and drive to deeper meaning and understanding.

The board member makes the interesting suggestion that for the first half year, perhaps, we should let students just explore the array of topics they might study, and then they can choose the one that most appeals to them. Perhaps, many teachers might think, students themselves could develop a list of topics. They might brainstorm thirty things, or fifty, and the teacher can write them on the board. That might allow both some degree of arbitrariness, in that the students just brainstormed them, and also allow choice, as students choose the topics they prefer from the list.

I do think the earlier principle—about everything being interesting if we learn enough about it—trumps the belief that we should give the students choice. One possible problem with allowing choice is that students might then think that they should be able to choose something else if their first choice fails to satisfy them immediately or if they see that a friend is more immediately engaged with her topic. They might also be encouraged to think, if they find launching into their topic less interesting than they had hoped, that they are to blame for having made a bad choice.

Everyone knows from experience that what might be a favorite topic at age five will not likely still be a favorite at fifteen. Giving students a choice is not a reliable guide to their future interest in that topic. Commonly children will express a particular interest in something that they saw in a movie a week ago or that someone mentioned yesterday, and such interests are commonly evanescent. The topics we will have chosen for them will have qualities that encourage continued interest and development of under-standing that their favorite five-year-old choice might not have. Even giving them a choice within the set of brainstormed topics is also vulnerable to the other objections given here.

I do recognize that this notion of giving students no choice runs counter to an almost universally held principle. Being almost universally held doesn't make it right, of course. And I should, again, qualify the claim that "everything" is interesting if learned in enough depth. In chapter 4 I will explore the ways I'd qualify that, and how we might select topics that will have the features necessary for this proposal to work. It might also be worth recall-ing that we actually give students choice in hardly anything of importance in schooling, beginning with whether they'd like to attend or not. We don't ask for a show of hands about who would like to do algebra or learn about the French Revolution, and so on. We tend to reserve choice to things of little value, as a kind of cosmetic suggestion that they have choice where in fact we al-low them little; it helps to disguise from those of us complicit in schooling the coercive nature of the institution.

In general, then, I think there are many virtues to the random-ness of the topics and that introducing choice is fraught with problems. But I don't want to be too dogmatic about this. If, for some good reason, a student should find a particular topic is seri-ously unsatisfying or disturbing or problematic in some way, then of course they can be allowed to change to another topic. But I anticipate such occasions being rare, and requiring a compel-ling reason. A teacher who has implemented the program took the set of recommended topics from the LiD Web site and, after discussions, allowed each child to choose three. The teacher then selected one of the three she thought would work best for each student: an interesting compromise.

The board member accurately described something that I think is common to many of us—a series of enthusiasms for topics that then shifted as something else captured his imagination. As I'll show in chapter 5, among the basic principles that will guide teachers in helping students explore their topics is that different kinds of enthusiasms will find a place at different ages in developing students' portfolios about a single topic. That is, each topic will be explored in multiple dimensions, artistically, physically, emotionally, academically, and so on. Rather than try to give examples here, I'll leave this to chapters 5 and 6, and hope you'll stick with me that long.

So I think that this proposal can quite easily accommodate the changing nature of what students might be interested in at different ages. Accommodating changing interests doesn't mean that a student has to flit from topic to topic. The aim is ever-increasing "inside-ness" and exploring the variety within each topic is an important part of that.

I worry a little about the claim that I have chosen what would mostly be considered academic and science topics, and have suggested predominately academic ways of exploring them. But perhaps I can put off that issue to chapter 4 as well, where I'll explore the kinds of topics that would work for this scheme. *Mothballs* will not make it to the list!

No doubt many might share the suggestion that students should be given a choice to continue with their topic or change it at, say, grade 8. Again, it is important to remember when considering these possibilities that no one has been through a program of study like this, so it is unwise to base expectations too much on current norms. My suspicion is that students will be very reluctant to change topics after their eight years of investment, when they are beginning to discover how little they know about something that has become full of wonder for them. Maybe they will not commonly use the five words made famous in a very different context by Charlton Heston, but I think the great majority of children's response to moving to a different topic and leaving the one they have been building their portfolio on will be more akin to prying it "from their cold dead hands." Those who might expect students to happily change to a different topic or drop the whole idea of Learning in Depth are reasonably basing their assumptions on how students today might greet an option to start something new, or stop something old. I think it is hard to imagine the mind-set that will be created by eight years of unforced but encouraged study of some specific topic. That being said, I suppose such an option might be allowed for some students. I do think it would begin to undermine the central purpose of building real expertise though.

A further point should be made about the reasonable desire that students should be able to follow and generate their own tastes and interests within the topic they are given. The portfolios are the students' after all. They are not for grading. The teacher initially will be important in helping students find sources, explore new dimensions they have not yet encountered, and so on. As time goes by, students will increasingly take control of the direction of their topics, using the teacher more as a sounding board, occasionally seeking advice, but generally letting their own interests determine the shape their portfolios take. For instance, a biology-inclined Sara might want to vigorously pursue apples and diseases; a culinary-inclined Sara, apples as food; a technically inclined Sara, the ultimate peeler/corer; an artistically inclined Sara, a file of apples in great paintings, with her own representations of apples; and so on. That is, the arbitrariness of the topic need not be seen as a complete constraint on students; rather the opposite—it opens them to a world of knowledge they would otherwise have had no idea of and allows them to explore dimensions of that knowledge driven by their own changing interests. I suppose this reflects the paradox of the constraining frame providing the freedom that allows the picture to be painted. A belief that drives this proposal, which is well attested by experience, is that students will be intrinsically motivated to elaborate their portfolios because of the imaginative engagement that develops with depth of knowledge—think of hobbies and collections.

I mentioned earlier the Project Method, which was promoted by Kilpatrick in the early part of the twentieth century (e.g., Kilpatrick 1918), and ably continued today, prominently led by Lilian G. Katz and Sylvia C. Chard. In discussing the choice of topics,

Katz and Chard (1998a, 1998b) give four reasons for not giving in to the assumption that student choice is crucial. Their reasons overlap somewhat with those given above:

> Using children's interests as a starting point in topic selection may lead to choosing appropriate topics, but this approach also presents several potential pitfalls. First, what does it mean to say that an individual or group of children is "interested" in a topic? Interests can be of relatively low educational value; [one researcher] gives the example of a young boy in his class whose main "interest" for some time was how to pull off the legs of a fly! Children's interests may actually represent passing thoughts, fleeting concerns, phobias, obsessions, or fascination with media-related characters.
>
> Second, just because children express interest in a given topic does not mean that their interest deserves to be strengthened by the serious attention of the teacher. For example, the publicity given to movies may provoke children's interest in a certain topic. . . . In other words, we suggest making a distinction between providing opportunity for child-initiated spontaneous activity about a topic and investing in a long-range effort focused on it.
>
> Third, one of the responsibilities of adults is to help children to develop new intellectual interests. Children's awareness of their teacher's real and deep interest in a topic worthy of their investigation, for example, can stimulate their own interest in the topic as well.
>
> Fourth, we suggest that a topic should reflect our commitment to taking children and their intellectual powers seriously, and to treating children as serious investigators. It is easy to underestimate the satisfaction and meaning children gain from the hard work of close observation of nearby phenomena.

Objection 3. The students will drop out or revolt against it.

A vice-principal of a city high school. She taught social studies in middle-schools for ten years, then did a masters degree in counseling, and worked for another ten years in that role in the school at which she holds her current position.

From my experience dealing with adolescents for a long time, I'd say that, even if you can keep young children engaged with a topic for six or seven years or so, once adolescence hits, this thing that has been a part of their lives so long—tied up with their school, teachers, parents, if they have been supportive of the topic—will come to represent an imposed authority's task, and they will, in droves would be my bet, revolt against it. Threats and bribery—in the mild forms we use these in school systems—may keep them at it for their early years, but for most students it will become irksome and be seen as drudgery. I think they will vote with their feet, and stop adding anything to their portfolio. The less dramatic of them will not revolt in any obvious way, but you'll see they will simply pretend to add to the portfolio, but won't actually do anything much with it.

I am skeptical that you could get them to stay with it to adolescence—though maybe adding choice and flexibility might help a bit—but I'm confident that it would not survive the disturbances of adolescence, and I'm confident it would be seen as a prime target against which revolt can be directed. The fact that they have been doing it for so many years, and that it will be seen as valuable by teachers and maybe parents, makes it even more useful as a symbol of what they want to revolt against; by revolting against it, and what is seen as its value, they will be able to provoke the kind of reaction so many adolescents crave at this age.

Well, that's my view based on the psychology of the students I have known over many years. What makes this even less likely to hold them is the fact that this isn't to be graded in any way. Now students coming to the last few years of high school are under a lot of pressure. They don't have time for all their schoolwork demands anyway, and if something is going to be squeezed out, it won't be what they need for their coming exams. Their ungraded portfolio about *grass* or *birds* or whatever is what'll take the hit.

I agree with much that my colleagues have said. I'm particularly concerned about how this fits into other parts of the curriculum. In one form or another, everything done in schools is evaluated.

While everyone knows it's not the best motivator, at least grading provides both a check on how well we and the student are doing in anything we teach, and it does provide a continuing motivator for students to learn. If there were no testing in schools, how much learning do you think would take place? And you expect us to implement a proposal that will run from K to 12 without any incentive to keep the students involved in developing their portfolios except what you imagine will be the pleasure of doing it. I can only conclude that you are very very optimistic! There will never be sufficient motivation to keep students at it.

If we tried to implement this project without any sanctions against students who drop out, what do you expect to happen? And if they start dropping out, what do you do then? It will only take one or two kids to give up, and the rest will begin to see that they don't need to keep this going, and you will face mass defection from the scheme.

If this were a reasonable idea that could have the impact you are suggesting, it would have been tried before somewhere. If it had worked, it would be in practice everywhere. I don't think it's worth supporting even a pilot project.

Response to: The students will drop out or revolt against it.

The vice-principal begins with adolescents, assuming that would be the age at which this project would most likely come adrift, even if it manages to survive that long. And, indeed, the accommodations with the adult world that adolescents make are never entirely easy, and in many cases lead to various forms of resistance to and revolt against the norms they are expected to conform with. Will this area of rapidly deepening and enriching knowledge become something students revolt against? "I've had enough of damn apples! trees! railways! leaves!" Much more likely, I think, is that their topics will provide an area of recourse and solace to the alienated youth. People might let them down, institutions might hem them in, but you can always rely on *trees/apples/railways!* Well, that puts it in joke form, but there are better grounds to expect that students will cling to their area of growing expertise—which by the teen years will be a much more formidable resource than almost any student attains in schools today—than that they will discard it.

The expectation that their portfolio and topic will serve them as a refuge from the disturbances of adolescence rather than become a target for their revolt is, of course, impossible to argue convincingly. Only experience will sort this out for us. All I can do here is suggest that the outcome the vice-principal predicts may not turn out to be the commonest result. No doubt we may see some cases of both kinds of response by different students, and it is a potential danger that we should be prepared for. I do take her objection seriously, and in chapter 5 I will describe some steps we can take to minimize its potential force. I think it is reasonable to expect that the continuing connection to their topics year after year will provide most students with a significant intellectual anchor amid the changing classes, schools, teachers, subject focuses, and so on, of their regular school lives.

I do want to defend the idea that the portfolios students compose should not be graded or evaluated, except in the informal way the supervising teacher will keep a watching brief on its development. The portfolios are monitored to help the student keep deepening their knowledge, but no one will be graded on how well he or she is doing. Building the portfolio is something that will be done for its own sake. The current orthodoxy that everything that is done in schools must be evaluated, or else how can you know whether it is being done adequately, is odd if you accept that education is largely a field of values and meanings—which we can't evaluate with any precision. So we evaluate other things, which are supposed to be connected with the values and meanings, and then we attend only to the other things and forget the values and meanings. Well, regardless of how seriously one takes such a critique, it would seem at least an interesting experiment to introduce into the curriculum a wholly uncoerced activity aimed at intensive learning, just to see whether it might not disconfirm what is currently taken for granted.

We don't evaluate our children's out-of-school reading—if they read—nor do we evaluate their hobbies nor their Facebook contributions, yet they often engage in such activities with great enthusiasm and energy, and learn a lot in doing so. The notion that evaluating is important as a source of motivation cannot be ignored, except of course its proponents do tend to ignore the problems associated with using evaluation as a motivator. If we told our children they *had* to collect keys or seashells or stones or postage stamps, or that they *had* to spend an hour on Facebook each day, the vice-principal might reasonably point out that because there will be no evaluation then we should not expect children to engage in such activities. And yet they do, even without our telling them to do it or rewarding them for doing it or punishing them for not doing it well enough. Indeed, nearly all children begin a collection or a hobby about age seven. What's going on? Why is this happening? We have an almost universal, spontaneous, intellectually engaging activity going on en masse, and where are the educational studies about hobbies and collecting? The fact that it is so nearly universal a phenomenon of childhood suggests that these portfolios on single topics have immense sources of energy to draw on if we present them properly. The experience of teachers who have begun pilot LiD projects so far has been, to the surprise of many of them, that the students were entirely unbothered by having a topic randomly ascribed, and began immediately and with some enthusiasm to associate with it, as their own. (This was less true of the implementations that began with grade 6 and 7 students, where they felt that giving the students choice was significant in their engagement with their topics.)

If some students become fed up with their portfolios and want to stop, what should we do? Nothing. Let them. This is something added to the curriculum, and if some students do not want it, there should be no compulsion to make them continue. My suspicion is that dropping out will be much rarer than people accustomed to current schooling expect. Also I suspect that after some months or a year without touching their portfolios dropout students will perhaps by chance discover something about their topic that will stimulate them to begin again, even if only desultorily at first. The enthusiasm of other students, the developing portfolios they see, and the interesting presentations will also likely put pressure on dropouts to drop back in again. Only experience will tell.

John Dewey wrote eloquently about the energy children bring to unforced learning whereas the "formal" stuff of schooling, subject to grading and all the rest, so often remains strangely repellent to so many (Dewey 1966, pp. 7–8). A teacher I worked with a few years ago observed: "I've noticed how some kids just let details go in one ear and out the other. Yet those same kids, if it is something they are truly interested in . . . will collect information for months and months and have every little bit of it emblazoned in their memories. I would guess that in broad topics there would be some specific area that each student would be interested in collecting details about, and especially if they could organize it as though it were a 'collection'" (with thanks to Susan Zucherman).

(But I haven't addressed the question of how we can know this scheme is successful if we don't have tight evaluation procedures in place to measure each child's degree of attainment of the indicators of success that will have to be established clearly before such a proposal can be accepted. It makes better sense to discuss this below in the response to the next question.)

There is also the objection that LiD would already have been put into practice somewhere if the proposed idea were any good. While this is a useful notion to weed out clearly eccentric ideas, it also weeds out *all* new ideas, good or bad. That no one has ever tried this before should properly give us pause, but it shouldn't stop us thinking about and evaluating such new ideas. I hope its novelty won't be too great a problem to its receiving a fair examination of its plausibility.

The vice-principal also makes the strong objection that later in high school, with the pressure of exams, of entertainment activities and social lives, and all the rest of what overfills typical teenagers' days and nights, something will have to give, and what will give for many of them, if not most, will be their LiD portfolios. This may prove true, but this is an objection that takes current conditions as still holding after Learning in Depth programs will have been in place for a decade or so. I think these programs will transform our schools and students more profoundly than the vice-principal imagines. She sees it as just another activity that will go by the wayside because of all the more attractive and more powerfully compelling things (like exams) that students will have in their lives. My suspicion is, to use the Heston phrase again, that students' response to leaving aside their portfolio development will be more like "you'll have to pry it from my cold, dead hands" than the casual dropping out that the vice-principal expects. I think that the attraction of the LiD portfolio will be powerful for most students. And even if they have to ease off in adding to it while they face exams, there is nothing lost. Again, only experience will decide such issues, but I think there are enough reasons to make it worthwhile to give LiD a try.

Objection 4. It would be too complicated to organize.
The chair of the Planning and Facilities Committee. He has an Ed.D. in educational leadership and worked in the Department of Education for five years before returning to his current senior administrative job in the school district.

The problems of running a complex scheme like this will be enormous, especially in times when kids are constantly changing schools, moving from region to region. How will anyone keep up with the array of portfolio topics all the kids are studying? And how do you propose noting this on their graduation? Can students fail their "in depth" study? By not going deep enough? How deep is deep enough? And if you aren't going to grade it, how do you indicate that the student who has worked passionately and imaginatively for twelve years has done any better than the kid who has sloppily created a garbage portfolio? Or are we supposed to think they'll all be wonderful?

This proposal looks innocent enough the way you described it, but it will become a nightmare to implement and keep track of. I'm imagining scenarios in which some kid at grade 3, studying *leaves*, moves to another city. In the new school a teacher has to be assigned to supervise this growing portfolio, and catch up on the topic herself so she can offer reasonable guidance. How is that to be financed? Then, two years later, the kid moves to yet another school, and we have more problems. Do the teachers in the schools the kid left get a reduction in salary? Your idea might seem easy enough when you think of a single student who stays in the same area for most of her schooling, but remember, we'll have literally hundreds of thousands of students moving from school to school across the country, and some will go abroad for a year, or two, or more. Do we cancel the portfolio if they go to a country that doesn't provide support for it? So you've got disconnects between grades, really big ones between different schools, and between primary/intermediate and secondary schools, and varying degrees of interest and connection from teachers as the kids stagger on with their topic—it's a logistical nightmare.

How many portfolios is one teacher supposed to help with? Suppose that, for each teacher a school will have, say, thirty students. That means each teacher will have to somehow keep up with thirty portfolios, and they meet each student at least an hour per month—that's more than one each day to deal with. Or do you imagine hiring teachers who will be solely concerned with these portfolios? What would that cost across the district? If, as my colleague has just noted, in the early years, students will have to interact with teachers maybe once a week or more, that's getting in the region of five or six a day for each teacher. They'll have no time to do anything else.

Also preparing units of study on any topic is very time consuming, and this program seems to require the teachers to prepare materials and units of study for more than twenty or thirty different topics. Impossible.

Sorry. Nice idea but no one did the math. It's just not practical.

Response to: It would be too complicated to organize.

I think the first set of issues raised by the chair of the Planning and Facilities Committee—about students moving from school to school, leaving the country for some time, etc.—is manageable. It will require resources and skill to make this scheme work, of course. But to suggest canceling it for reasons such as those would be a case of the administrative tail wagging the educational dog. If it is educationally desirable, then we make it possible. It really doesn't represent such a challenge. The teachers do not need to be experts in all the topics. The teachers need only be able to make suggestions, help the students reflect on their topic, and be good at finding information and suggesting directions for the student to pursue. They will need also to be sensitive to the kind of understanding students are developing at particular ages, and attuned to helping them see aspects of their topic in appropriate forms—I'll discuss this in some detail in chapter 5. As the years pass, the teachers will increasingly become sounding boards, and the students will have their own sense of directions—and the directions will be elaborating endlessly for them. Students moving from advisor to advisor should create no more problems than currently are caused by grade and teacher changes in schools. And for many students, parents or other older caregivers might provide continuity.

For the most part, such a curriculum innovation should not be particularly costly. Indeed, for a major educational innovation, its costs will be negligible. This doesn't require a complex bureaucracy. We don't even need any major changes to teacher education programs to accommodate this—maybe a workshop or two on how to support students' portfolio development would be sufficient, along with written guides incorporating an elaborated form of the contents of chapter 5.

But the suggestion that the proposal can't work because the teacher-student ratio makes it impossible does need to be considered in detail. I think we might usefully distinguish three distinct phases for the proposal. The first involves the beginning years of the scheme, when students are between ages five and eight, roughly. It is during this period that the chair's calculations are potentially most damaging. The second is from around age eight to about fourteen or fifteen. And the third is from then to the end of high school. In the third phase, I imagine the students will be working largely independently, with brief check-ins with their supervising teacher once each month. Much the same, with the check-ins taking a little more time, will also be adequate for the second phase—though there may be calls on time and resources beyond what can be accommodated within current budgets.

The serious problem comes with the beginning of the scheme, during the first three or four years. Even if we accept that each student's portfolio can begin to be put together at a relatively leisurely pace and we don't expect them to become any kind of experts in their first three years, we are still faced with one teacher having somehow to provide adequate support for between twenty and thirty students. And if we want consultations with the teacher to take place more than once each month, and perhaps as much as once each week or more, how can we manage this without hiring many more teachers? What kind of time commitment are we looking at? I think we could indeed manage the one consultation a month without too much difficulty. But, if it is to be once per week, and we have thirty students, and each student is given close attention for half an hour per week, that's fifteen hours of instruction time to be provided. If the teacher deals with three students at a time, giving each of them concentrated attention for around seven or eight minutes and discussing general and common problems or issues together, we still need to add five hours in the week. An average of seven or eight minutes each student per week may be adequate, though there wouldn't be much time for extensive discussion and appreciation. Taking the last hour of each day, with three students in each half hour, would enable a single teacher to deal with thirty students, seeing each one once per week. This would cost some money, and would be too great an additional burden on already stressed teachers.

But there are other ways of addressing the problem. Say we have only a limited number of appropriate topics, such that in any school topics will recur every third or fourth year. That means that a student beginning school may be given the topic *apples*. But some other student in grade 3 may also have been building a portfolio on *apples*, as will a student in grade 6, and, in nearby schools, perhaps, there will be students in grades 7 and 11, all of whom are building portfolios on *apples*. The students from the higher grades can supply some of the guidance, relieving the time costs on teachers, and also enriching "intergenerational" contacts among students. I should emphasize this part of the proposal more. Anyone involved in education knows how much nearly all older students enjoy teaching younger ones. Even older students who are not "high achievers" will nevertheless be able to give really significant help to young students setting out on a topic. If this project becomes quite widely implemented, one of its generally recognized benefits will be the intergenerational contacts between older and younger students, in which the older play an important role doing something that will be valued by the younger children and by the institution. This is one of a number of collateral benefits this proposal will bring to schooling.

These students will also become efficient users of the Internet, and may well be able to organize themselves somewhat. Indeed, it is hard to imagine this scheme existing for many years before there will be large networks of *apple* or *bird* enthusiasts with their own Web sites attracting people from any areas in which this project might become common. There will no doubt be the equivalents of Facebook networks formed, with hub pages around which students can communicate.

For the first three years in which students are beginning to build their portfolios we may find school librarians—where these are available—can also play a useful role. They and parent volunteers—where these are available—can also relieve the pressure on teachers' time. In addition, at some cost, it might become a common job for college students, and especially preservice teachers, to give some time to helping out early grade students in building their portfolios. These college students would also bring further benefits not unlike those we might expect from older school students helping out. And, of course, meeting with someone other than their regular teacher about their portfolios would add to students' sense of their "specialness."

These options for relieving the pressure on teachers' time hardly dissolve our problems of resources and time, but they do suggest that there are some resources we can use and redeploy without significant additional costs, and so we can make some headway against the stark impossibility conclusion that the chair suggests. It will call for some reallocating of resources, in terms of teachers' activities, supervising the students not being dealt with by the teacher, and shifting some curriculum time from other subjects to the LiD program.

When I was discussing this problem of time with a primary school staff recently, the principal interrupted to say that they have to spend a lot of time with mandated literacy activities, and are using many programs and drills that she finds bore the students and teachers and yield marginal results. She said that she would prefer to stop some of those activities in favor of LiD, with the expectation that the degree of interest LiD would stimulate in the students would likely lead to greater increases in their literacy scores than the exercises and drills that it would replace. I didn't argue with her, though I realize some would.

In a worst case scenario, if the above kinds of attempts to respond to the stark mathematics of the chair's objection still can't make the scheme administratively manageable, then perhaps we should accept that an increase in the number of teachers for the first three years of the scheme might be necessary. This would be a significant cost, but the promised return suggests that this might be an excellent educational investment. One half-time teacher could make the scheme workable. Alternatively, if school time and teachers' time are "full," then LiD will have to be considered in competition with other activities in the school, in terms of educational value. If everything that is currently being done is considered more educationally valuable than LiD, then this innovation will not be tried. If LiD is considered to be potentially of greater value than some current activities, then something will have to give way for it. These kinds of decisions are up to the teachers and administrators in particular places and circumstances to make. But they can be made, and they can enable LiD to be implemented at the cost of some other program or activity that currently takes teachers' and school time. This kind of choice faces teachers and administrators constantly, so, again, considering how to accommodate a new and potentially valuable program needn't be the impossibility suggested.

I should perhaps add that my response so far assumes that the chair's claim that this must be an add-on to the current demands made on teachers is not proving to be the case with a number of the schools that have so far mounted pilot projects. To my surprise, in the first schools to express an interest in LiD the problem of finding time and support for it has actually proved to be no problem at all. These are schools that had already built into their timetables a section for alternate activities. Many schools have slots for something like "Challenge Time" or "Exploration Time." In the schools attracted to LiD, the administrators and teachers have decided to dedicate some of that time to the pilot project for its initial three years. In one school, it was decided to take a chunk of the twice-weekly "Library" time block for work with portfolios; in another, it was deemed appropriate to take time allotted for "Enrichment Activities." That is, in all these cases the LiD project was able to run with no additional time demands placed on teachers. In most cases, the teachers were delighted to devote these times already committed to some form of enrichment activities. As students worked on their portfolios, the teacher was able to chat with them in turn to see what they were doing and make suggestions. The LiD project seemed to strike the teachers as a more attractive activity for them than previous uses of those time slots in the curriculum. As one superintendent put it rather brusquely: "We do lots of things in schools. They aren't all of equal educational value. We've discussed this and like its possibilities for our kids, so we are going to stop some other things and spend the time on getting LiD going."

I don't want to underestimate the difficulties that might be involved in implementing this proposal, but none of them that I can foresee makes excessive demands on finances, management, teachers' time, and so on. There may be some demands on all of these, but the potential payoff is out of proportion to any likely costs, and very small in the context of school system budgets. Rather than elaborate further on this here, I will return to it later when showing how we can implement the program in schools today.

One other point, in an overly long answer to a challenging question, is to note that much of the LiD work on topics will be done out of school. School time is required largely for relatively brief teacher discussions with the students about how the portfolio is developing, looking at recent additions, making suggestions for further directions the student might explore, or encouraging the student to elaborate on something already in the portfolio, etc. Work on portfolios, that is, will not make a demand on class time, except perhaps in those cases where some students finish a piece of class work early and can be invited to get on with doing something for their portfolio while the other students catch up. School libraries, too, of course, can provide a school space for portfolio work.

I am conscious that this response may suggest I am insufficiently aware of the daily realities of many elementary classrooms. The way I have described the program may make it seem to require skills and abilities many children simply don't have. Even getting them to attend to their topic consistently, and remember it, and begin to see how they might add things to their portfolios will sometimes require a great deal of teacher attention and work for very many students. So I need to acknowledge that in some schools and with some children this concern that I underestimate the difficulties of starting and the time it will take to get the program off the ground is well founded, and LiD will require more support than is suggested above. The question, then, for the administrator and teacher is the same that is faced by others: is it worth the effort and time and expense required? After all, the problem faced by LiD with regard to such children is no different than is faced in every other area of the curriculum. LiD won't solve the learning problems of such children, but it might provide them with a resource their current schoolwork fails to give them.

One final point: The chair's last concern—about the teacher having to prepare units of study for every topic—is a result of misunderstanding the way LiD works. The LiD supervisor will not be *teaching* these topics. Rather they will be helping students to begin exploring them. And there is no hurry, as there might be on a unit that has to be covered in, say, three weeks, when there is going to be a test to make sure the students have learned sets of skills and attained the knowledge objectives, and so on. The LiD supervisor will need to ensure there are resources the students can go to in order to discover something more about their topics, but they won't be required to prepare lessons on them. The LiD Web sites will, nevertheless, provide age-appropriate materials teachers might give to students in cases where local resources seem inadequate to keep the student going on some specific topic.

Objection 5. There's no adequate research basis for the
    proposal.
A university professor in educational psychology. He took a two-year
leave from his position after he won election to the school board.

This reminds me of curriculum-making a hundred or two hundred years ago. It comes as someone's bright idea, saying, "Hey! This might work. It'll transform everything. Implement it tomorrow!" It's pure speculation, armchair theorizing, with not a shred of evidence to support it. There's not even a pilot project, and here you are recommending we put this into the schools.

We are in an era when we have got beyond taking on board any madcap idea. We require sound evidence that any new practices introduced into schools are based on studies demonstrating that they can achieve sound educational objectives. This idea comes out of the blue, and seems to be based on nothing other than your claims about deep knowledge spreading some vague understanding to everything else one knows. It sounds to me like an optimistic fantasy. I want evidence that it will work before I'm willing to introduce it to my school system.

To make matters worse you don't even suggest that we should build in some evaluative procedures, to see if it does achieve its objectives. And to make things even worse than that, it doesn't have in it any objectives that we could evaluate. What's the point of introducing a distinct and elaborate new practice when we have no way of telling whether it works, or even know what "working" would amount to?

I mean, what counts as success for this scheme? Just the fact that it is running? We need something more than that before we impose it on children. You need to take this back to your study or armchair and come up with something that enters the era of scientific research in education. We need a much more precise proposal, a series of clearly articulated objectives each of which is amenable to rigorous testing, a description of the assessment procedures that will be used, evidence that it can deliver on these objectives, and so on. You should take a few introductory educational psychology courses to see how to design a study and do basic research in education, then come back with something that uses a scientific approach to the problem you are supposedly addressing.

Response to: There's no adequate research basis for the proposal.

Making decisions about what should constitute the curriculum is very largely a matter of values and meanings. Faced with a proposal like this we have to assess whether and how much we value the likely results of such a component of an educational program. We have to consider whether a person who has been through such a program better represents what we mean when we use the term "educated" than is common for today's typical graduates. These

are not empirical questions we can work out some scientific test
to determine for us. These are questions of meanings and values.

Consider what is the evidence that justifies the inclusion of social studies in the curriculum? Decisions to include such curriculum components do not turn on empirical questions. Whether to
include the social studies in the curriculum, or the Learning in
Depth program, turns not on some empirical evidence that might
be brought to bear, but on whether one's conception of education is better realized by such components. There may be empirical questions about how best to implement them, but the main
questions we have to deal with here are questions of meaning: is
education improved by this addition in your analysis?—and questions of value: is this a better instantiation of your conception of
education?

This demand for evidence of a specific kind is a little like the
old attempts to research whether discovery methods of teaching
or straightforward didactic methods were more efficient. More
efficient at what? The trouble was that progressivists did not favor
discovery-learning methods because they were the most efficient
at ensuring memorization and retention of knowledge. Even if
one could show empirically that they were less effective than didactic methods or, say, some new subliminal drill technique, that
finding would be beside the educational point. Progressivists favor
such methods because they embody the qualities that are a part of
the progressivist conception of education. Similarly, Learning in
Depth is a proposal to be evaluated in terms of its adequacy as a
constituent of a particular educational ideal. That is to be decided
not by some technical method but by, well, thinking. Armchairs
are quite good places to do that. That's a little too glib, perhaps, so
I will return to this issue at greater length in Appendix A.

What counts as success for such a scheme? Consider again a
comparison with the social studies curriculum. How do you evaluate the success that justifies its current place in the curriculum?
Where is the evidence that the social studies are successful in
creating the kind of responsible citizen they are supposed to generate? And how do we compare adequacy of citizenship among

countries that have the social studies as a prominent element in their curricula with those that don't? Similarly, Learning in Depth aims to produce in a distinctive way a more knowledgeable person, but we have to decide whether or not to include this new element in the curriculum on the basis of whether this kind of person is in harmony with what we mean by education, and on the basis of the reasons given for believing that it is likely to attain the end described—as a kind of person, not some product.

The Learning in Depth proposal is not *speculation*. It isn't some kind of guess about educating that is uninformed by relevant empirical findings. The value of an educational theory comes from the adequacy of the image it generates of the educated person and the analysis of the logical entailments of such an image for the curriculum. The proposal to introduce Learning in Depth is not some claim to be more efficient at reaching some agreed aim in education, but it is rather a proposal for changing the meaning of "education" a little. It is an attempt to generate an image of how we might achieve a more adequate form of education.

But how are we to tell whether it is successful? Well, there are a number of fairly gross measures that we can apply initially. Do the students get bored and drop out in significant numbers? Do students typically begin to build adequate portfolios and increasingly become interested in their topics? How difficult is it to get the students underway? How much time is required to support each student? Are most portfolios adequate in the sense of gathering significant amounts of information; do students classify the information well enough for clear understanding, and reclassify the information as it grows in volume? Are the students sufficiently enthusiastic that they spend more time building their portfolios than is required to make minimal responses to teachers' suggestions? Are the students making discoveries of information by their own efforts and recording them in ways that their supervising teachers and others can understand? To what degree are their year-end presentations clear, interesting, and well organized? Do the students give evidence of imaginative engagement with their topics? How adequately can other school resources—teacher-librarians, parent volunteers, older students—provide assistance? Is it better to begin the project in kindergarten, grade 1, grade 3, or grade 7? Is such unassessed study adequately motivating?

One way to begin researching this project would be to run a three-year implementation in two or three classes in each of half a dozen schools in widely different socioeconomic neighborhoods and conduct a series of assessments throughout the program and at the conclusion of the three years. One would want to test whether students had indeed learned a lot about their topics and whether they were interested in continuing with them, and one would also look for insights from their teachers and from parents about how well the program was conforming to some of the claims made in this book.

So, despite my claim that mostly one would choose to implement a program like this on the basis of thinking about how well or otherwise it furthers one's educational values, some fairly simple and gross assessments could also be put in place to get measures of its success or otherwise at meeting some of the objectives set out in this book for the program. It would not be a matter of announcing success simply because the program is running, and it isn't as though the program has no objectives beyond its existence in a school. This book lays out a number of objectives for learning in depth.

Objection 6. This proposal violates nearly everything we know about young children as learners.

An elementary school teacher. She taught for nine years, earned a Ph.D. in early childhood education, and served on the Research Committee of the school board for five years.

Often there are good reasons why some educational idea has never been tried before! One is that it's in conflict with what we know about children's intellectual development. Young children are concrete thinkers, and they need to begin with topics that are part of their everyday experience. We make sure that any new topics we introduce are tied in with what the children already know.

If you just give them some random topic, like *beetles* or *the circus* or *spices,* they will have no concrete experience to connect them with the topic, and so it won't mean anything to them.

This is also a very traditionalist proposal: content is everything and the children are nowhere—education as knowledge accumulation. If we learned anything in the twentieth century, it was that children's early education needs to first attend to the child. We have learned to ask, first, what are the needs of the child? Do the child's needs include beginning to learn a massive amount of information about *leaves* or *apples?* Of course not. This introduces a new curriculum item that treats children's minds as nothing other than knowledge repositories.

One of the strong and proven principles we have worked with for some time is that you should involve children in planning their learning. This proposal violates that principle by imposing a topic on children and doesn't even invite them to choose what might interest them. We also give great emphasis to recognizing the different needs of different students, and also being attuned to their particular intelligences. This proposal violates that principle by treating all children the same and simply dropping a random topic on each one.

You wouldn't be able to get the average five-year-old interested in *leaves,* or *spiders,* or even *apples* sufficiently to get the process going successfully. Another central principle for early learning is that children need hands-on experience with whatever they are learning. I'm not sure how you plan for this with *the circus,* or many of your other topics. No accommodation seems to be made to the principles that we now know determine successful learning in young children.

In young children learning is also a cooperative matter, and this proposal allows for only occasional cooperation. Mostly the student works alone, building a portfolio that is uniquely his or hers, and no one else is involved with it, except the various advising teachers and perhaps parents and sometimes others who might have the same topic. Also we think of knowledge as something that is drawn out of students rather than as information that is imposed on them. In fact, there is hardly a principle of early learning I can think of that this proposal doesn't violate.

When I say that it is largely hopeless because it is consistently developmentally inappropriate I should elaborate what I mean. The concept of developmental appropriateness has three dimensions: age appropriateness, individual appropriateness, and cultural appropriateness. Age appropriateness is based on research—much of it on Piaget's well-known theories of children's development—which indicates that there are universal, predictable sequences of growth and change that occur in children during the first nine years of life. Your proposal is made as though all the findings of this research don't exist. Individual appropriateness recognizes that each child is a unique person with an individual pattern and timing of growth, as well as an individual personality, learning style, and family background. No recognition of this is made in the proposal. Cultural appropriateness recognizes the importance of the knowledge of the social and cultural contexts in which children live to ensure that learning experiences are meaningful, relevant, and respectful for the children and their families. Your proposal is simply concerned with knowledge accumulation, and some belief that it will magically solve our problems, and it ignores all the features of being culturally appropriate to students.

It seems pointless to go on, but I should add that a lot of my work of late has been devoted to developing more meaningful integrated curricula for our students. This proposal goes in the opposite direction.

*Response to: This proposal violates nearly everything we know
    about young children as learners.*

A number of the theories and principles that currently dominate thinking about education during the early years of schooling are quite odd. We do see the world, and children, through the theories we adopt or unconsciously inherit, and if one adopts or inherits a theory that claims children are concrete thinkers able to learn only about everyday experience and local environments, then that's what one will see when one looks at children. I am sure that in a decade or so people will look back and wonder at how anyone could have believed such extraordinary things about children—in much the way that educational researchers today look back a few decades and wonder how anyone could have believed the tenets of behaviorism. How can one talk with a child for more than ten minutes and conclude that they are "concrete thinkers"? How can one look at what they become intellectually most excited by and conclude that their minds are somehow constrained by local experience and environments? Nearly all the young children I know are fascinated with dinosaurs, wicked witches, spies, star warriors, and seriously weird pop stars.

The stories that most engage the children I know involve Grimm fairy tales and *Where the Wild Things Are*. These are all stories built on battles between fear and security, courage and cowardice, good and evil, etc. Children use such concepts all the time in their thinking and speaking. Human beings never learn more *abstract* concepts in their lives.

So I am unworried by the board member's conviction that my proposal runs in the face of such current orthodoxies of childhood education. (Though I am not convinced the project needs to be conceptualized in such a manner; one could imagine accepting all those ideas and still implementing this project quite straightforwardly.) Nor am I concerned that she characterizes the program as stuffing knowledge into children's minds, making them merely repositories of meaningless data. I am, after all, addressing a problem of ignorance, and it must always be a bit hard for someone proposing principles of education to find herself, as this board member seems to be, defending ignorance. Well, that's maybe a bit unfair (I hear you howl), and what she is concerned to prevent is simply having students accumulate masses of meaningless knowledge. But building portfolios is not merely a matter of stuffing in one chunk of knowledge after another. In chapter 5 I will elaborate on the principles that govern how we can help students construct portfolios that will grow in depth and richness of understanding as they accumulate knowledge.

The board member seems convinced that there is no way to get children interested in such topics as *leaves, the solar system,* or *apples.* But such convictions flow from theories of what is "developmentally appropriate" that seem to me fundamentally flawed. (I have tried elsewhere [Egan 2002] to show where these theories came from and how they developed into their current forms, and what was and is wrong with them.)

Having got that off my chest, I will try, in chapter 5, to allay her fears that this proposal is developmentally inappropriate, and to show that there are good reasons to expect children will become increasingly committed to their portfolio topics as time goes on. I will try to show how students will be intimately involved in planning their own learning, can work cooperatively if they want, and can do all the things whose neglect she has inferred from her theoretical commitments. Another underlying principle of this project has been best stated by Jerome Bruner as "any subject can be taught effectively in some intellectually honest form to a child at any stage of development" (1960, p. 31).

Objection 7. This proposal won't deliver what it claims.

The longest serving member on the school board. He taught in Asia for a decade or so, and then in Europe. He completed an M.Ed. degree in educational leadership six years ago. He is recognized as a sound, commonsense realist, wary of theories and innovations.

My neighbor collects all kinds of stuff about 1950s cars. He has a garage full of the stuff. He knows every model ever built, all the varieties that were introduced during the decade, and he has these really neat files of service books, advertising materials, and even a huge collection of old car keys, each labeled with the kind of car it fitted. He's also really nerdy, and thick as all get out about everything else. He's a poster boy for your scheme, but is a walking disaster zone as a human being. His hobby acts as an escape for him, and doesn't provide all these wonderful benefits you suggest. In fact, if it wasn't for an allowance he's been drawing from his father's estate, I don't know how he'd survive. He hasn't held a job for years now.

Look, I can see that you are concerned about how our kids don't have a lot of academic knowledge when they leave school, but they know all kinds of other stuff. All these tests and people waving their arms about how the schools are failing and the kids are ignorant as all get out just leaves me cold. The kids today really impress me. The schools are turning out people with the skills this society needs right now. All this going to hell in a handcart stuff is usually touted by people wanting to turn the system back a hundred years. And that's how I see this proposal.

When kids don't know the Treaty of Versailles—hey, I don't know hardly anything about it!—academic types go crazy. But those same kids can do video stuff, and zip through the Internet, and deal with all kinds of technology easily. Leaves me breathless what they can do. I saw a video one class put together the other day, about global warming, and it was technically great and had all the information lined up. It was terrific. They put it on YouTube, in neat segments. And knowing about the Treaty of Versailles wouldn't add anything to it! And what's more relevant to them today? They are smart and skilled in the ways the world of tomorrow calls for, not in ways that suit how the world was a hundred years ago—and that's what this proposal is really about, preserving an old-fashioned education for an outdated world.

You say we've made a mistake in making the achievement of broad relevant knowledge our first priority for all students, and that most students do not gain an adequate sense of what knowledge is all about. You claim that some part of the solution is to give greater priority to learning in depth. You claim that the sense of the nature of knowledge learned in depth will "spread" to all the other knowledge students are exposed to. I see no reason to expect this. Your case for the value of this innovation turns on being able to show us, or persuade us, that this transfer will take place. If it doesn't, all we will have is the current situation about breadth of knowledge, made worse because of the time taken away from it for your proposal, and students knowing a great deal about something that is irrelevant to anything they will use in their everyday lives. Having huge knowledge about *apples* or *spiders* guarantees nothing about that person's educational attainments in general. It really is like what students would call a nerdy or geeky hobby. What evidence can you give us that the transfer you claim will occur will occur?

Response to: This proposal won't deliver what it claims.

It is clear that just accumulating knowledge isn't sufficient; it has to be certain kinds of knowledge. The board member is right that those who collect something endlessly or become immersed in football statistics don't have the right tool for the job. So maybe we need to revise that "anything"; not anything will do. So it makes matters a bit more difficult that not any kind of knowledge in depth can deliver these intellectual values. Knowing a massive amount about baseball or even cricket scores, or the lives of pop stars, or the contents of the *Guinness Book of Records* is unlikely to do the job for us. Certain kinds of knowledge, which I will describe in chapter 4, are required in order to deliver the benefits of learning in depth.

Most people who have learned something in significant depth—unless it is something quite trivial—find that they don't simply accumulate knowledge but also accumulate some understanding about knowledge in general. Even in the limited learning in depth that is common later in our current system, especially in universities, students begin to recognize that their sense of how to establish knowledge claims changes, and their new deeper learning impacts their previous knowledge. The simple confidence they had in the surface meaning of what they had earlier learned is challenged.

Now that is hardly an adequate refutation of the board member's objection to the proposal. Such questions will be definitively answered by practice, and now we can only look for the kind of evidence that would help us decide whether it is worthwhile implementing the proposal as a pilot project. The issue of "transfer" is complex, of course, particularly with regard to the kind of depth learning I am proposing. I think that most of the—admittedly imprecise—evidence we can see favors the expectation that there will be significant impacts from students' depth learning to everything else they know. I can hardly deny that some of the evidence suggests some people can learn in depth and gain no wider intellectual benefits from it. They can remain, in Montaigne's lovely phrase, "Asses loaded with books." But I think those are people who have not learned in depth in the way this program is set up to achieve, and, more important, the topics they have learned about in depth do not have the amplitude that the topics of this program will have. Further reasons for a little more optimism will be given in chapters 5 and 6, in the descriptions of how the project will be organized.

It is likely that learning something in depth will also lead students to transfer a whole range of learning strategies to other material they learn in school. That is, as students gather increasingly sophisticated knowledge and understanding about their topics they also learn strategies that can be applied to any other topic; the procedures they have used in their depth study will be available to use on anything else they need to learn. For example, if you have learned how it is possible to classify apples in a number of different ways—by size, color, nutritional value, shelf life, times of ripening, etc.—you will carry this understanding to help you organize other topics you will study, and if you have come to grasp the importance of preserving varieties of apples to protect against devastating disease, then you will be able to use that cognitive skill in looking at other food sources and other aspects of human behavior. So I think there are good reasons to expect students who undertake learning in depth to increasingly approach all learning in a different way.

A difficult part of arguing for this proposal is that we live in an educational world in which nothing quite like it has been done before. So it isn't easy to argue convincingly that it will work as advertised, especially when some of its features may seem to conflict with some currently dominant principles of educational thinking. We do have people around who have learned something in depth—the kind of specialists that fill our universities. But they are not examples of what I am arguing for. They have become specialists in an area of study for professional reasons, and usually only began to become specialists about the time this project reaches its conclusion, in grade 12. I am looking to make each child deeply knowledgeable about some very specific topic, and each child will be learning about it from age five or six until the end of their schooling. Because of the way I will recommend they can explore their topics, I think it is quite reasonable to expect the result of implementing this proposal will be minds somewhat unlike anything we commonly see today. Of course, there are some people who have serendipitously done something like this, and there is something important to admire about the results. But here is a proposal that this be made available to everyone, and the proposal is made with some confidence that the new mental development entailed by this proposal will indeed transfer or spread to the rest of the mental furniture each person carries in her or his mind.

We can make guesses, elaborate intuitions, spell out arguments, and interpret what evidence bears on the issue, as I am doing here. My hopeful suspicion is that the results in general might exceed even the optimistic predictions made in this book.

Objection 8. It isn't going anywhere without teacher buy-in, and it's not going to get it.

A senior official in the school board office. He has worked at the board office for twenty years. He first became a junior member of the school financing department, and has since become an expert in this area. He is currently in charge of marketing school district programs to other jurisdictions, especially internationally.

We've already drawn attention to the fact that this will be an added burden on teachers. It may have some features that some teachers like—nongraded, learning intensive, exploratory with no set boundaries and ministry guidelines, inviting students to become experts and technologically savvy with a purpose, possibly providing a strong incentive for individual learning. Mind you, a number of my colleagues have expressed skepticism about some of these expectations. But this proposal is going nowhere in the schools; even if we were all in favor of it, it would still hit the wall of teachers' hostility.

First you'll get the "one more thing to do" objection from overworked, educational-reform-fatigued teachers. You'll also find principals will be reluctant to promote it in the face of teachers' reluctance to try something new—and this is new with a vengeance. It's untried, and teachers won't be able to wrap their heads around it. Also the old "professional autonomy" card will be played, because teachers lose control of what and how students are learning in this scheme.

Response to: It isn't going anywhere without teacher buy-in, and it's not going to get it.

What is slightly funny about this objection is that, when I have described the idea of Learning in Depth to groups of teachers in schools or at teacher conventions, they are mostly (but far from invariably) enthusiastic but assure me it will be really difficult to get educational administrators behind it. The administrators tell me they are enthusiastic, but that teachers will never go for it. Indeed, most groups I have spoken to become in favor of it but assure me that it will hit the wall of some other group's hostility.

I think there are two reasons why we will only get a minimum of the "one more thing to do" objection from "overworked, educational-reform-fatigued teachers," as the official nicely puts it. First is that we will put in place support for teachers from parent volunteers, teacher-librarians, older students, college students, and some additional teachers if necessary. That is, implementing this program can't be simply on the backs of teachers. Other resources will have to be found, except in places where the whole staff agrees LiD is of sufficient priority to take up some "challenge time" already committed or to replace some other activity currently taking teachers' time. Second, the kind of nongraded, exploratory learning that students will be engaged with should be very attractive to most teachers. It is, as many have said to me, just what they got into teaching for, and currently have too little opportunity to do. A second-and-a-half reason a number of teachers have suggested is that this project will provide a convenient way of dealing with those classes in which the faster students are shouting "I'm done!" when most of the class is only part way into the task. The teacher can simply recommend that the faster students put in some time on their portfolio development.

Principals have been among the most enthusiastic groups. LiD would be an additional and significant program they can offer to parents as value added to their current curriculum. Nearly all principals I have spoken with have expressed concern only about resources to help their teachers take on another responsibility. Admittedly, I haven't spoken with a large number of principals, and the ones I have spoken with are maybe not representative. And I have spoken with a few principals who have been resolutely opposed to LiD for a variety of the reasons I have given in this chapter.

No one so far has played "the old 'professional autonomy' card." Indeed, it has not occurred to any of the teachers I have so far spoken to about this project, and I think there are enough attractive features of it for teachers that any concern about "professional autonomy" seems irrelevant.

Objection 9. The Internet will undermine this project.

A high school English teacher. He taught for fifteen years in an inner-city neighborhood, and then spent four years working as an associate instructor in a college teacher education program, mainly supervising preservice teachers. He is the school board's liaison officer concerned with credentialing teachers.

You've mentioned that you think students can start building both a physical portfolio of drawings, notes, pictures, articles, whatever, and also an online portfolio, for which they will be allotted space on a school or school district server. I think the Internet would undermine this idea in a number of ways. You'll get kids who go home with their topic, and a couple of days later a parent has downloaded fifty gigabytes of material on *apples* or *birds* and loaded it onto the student's server space. The student will have learned nothing, but they will have a huge portfolio. This will be true at the beginning of any students' project, and also throughout. The ease of access to knowledge now will mean your students are simply amassing material on topics, but they aren't gaining knowledge in depth about them.

You might want to have the teachers or supervisors of the portfolios play the role of gatekeepers, preventing students adding items to the portfolio unless they have "learned" them. But then you are back to assessment and testing, which you said you were excluding from this project. If a student studying *apples* has found an interesting account by an expedition to Kyrgyzstan that is studying parasites on the leaves of the original apple trees—to take one of your examples—and wants to include the sixty-eight-page PDF file in her online portfolio, what is the teacher supposed to do? Make sure the student has actually read it, and understands it? Allow her just to add it as a separate file among the hundreds she now has accumulated? Or does the teacher require her to reorganize her online portfolio every now and then, and show that she has an increasingly sophisticated understanding of the topic by how she structures the information she has gathered, such that the teacher accepts the new file only if the student shows she has a good sense of where it fits in her portfolio?

On the other hand, you'll have families and schools with hardly any Internet connections, so how are those students supposed to keep up with accumulating information?

My problem is that I can see this idea sounding really nice if you keep it pretty vague and general, but when you get down to the nitty-gritty of how it will actually work, there are just too many holes in it. And I think this Internet hole is just another big reason why the project won't work as you imagine and won't deliver the benefits you propose.

Response to: The Internet will undermine this project.

As some of the board member's examples suggest, the easy access to knowledge provided by the Internet can certainly enable students to build massive portfolios while completely evading the intent of this program. As in most cases where the letter of the law can be followed while the spirit is avoided, it is not easy to police the divide. If this program is seen in an uncompetitive way, in which the teachers' main role is to help students build their portfolios and the portfolios are ungraded and made up of what the students have learned, then it shouldn't be hard to make clear that amassing a huge amount of material in one's online space is simply irrelevant to what students are supposed to be doing. The built-in competitiveness of much modern schooling—at least from many parents' points of view—drives this objection in large degree. Remove the competitiveness and there is no incentive to amass data in the way suggested.

Parents or other caregivers will be important to helping, or hindering, the success of the project. It will be important to ensure that they understand what it is about, and how best they can support their child's exploration of their personal topic. An initial opportunity to explain the purposes of the program will come with the small ceremony at which the students are given their topics. Parents, caregivers, and other family members should be invited to the ceremony. They should also be given a brief booklet to take home that will outline the ways in which they can be most helpful in supporting their child's learning in depth of a specific topic.

A few people have suggested that the online component should, indeed, be dropped. That is, students should be allowed to use the Internet for their researches, but their portfolios would only be physical, rather than virtual, or analog rather than digital. This would make it easier to avoid the problems the board member points to, but it would also cut off a potentially valuable support to the project just to prevent an abuse. Such a constraint would also be unrealistic. We are currently living with so many constraints on our individual liberties brought about by attempts to constrain the actions of abusers of those liberties that I'd be reluctant to add yet another one. Better to work harder at making the positive part of the program work as intended. Some teachers, on the other hand, have argued for an online portfolio from the beginning. They suggested that it is now so easy to make digital pictures or copies of children's work and then store them online that they would do this routinely and would be able to help the children organize their files as time goes on. In discussion with teachers about this, there have been quite sharp divisions about the possibilities of the Internet and online storage of portfolio materials.

There might be a case for a modified form of the exclusionary policy some have suggested with regard to the Internet. Maybe for the first five or six years one might require the student's portfolio to take an exclusively physical form, and then provide the server space for online development in grade 5 or 6. The problem with this is that I think it would work less well for some topics than for others. Information about ubiquitous *dust* or about *the circus* might be harder to accumulate in a physical portfolio than, say, *leaves* or *birds*. I'm not at all sure about this, but the board member has clearly raised an important objection, overcoming which will require some subtlety. I will try to find some subtlety in chapter 6, where I'll discuss the form portfolios might take.

The other potential problem created by the Internet that must be acknowledged is that, if the program works as suggested and in a few years we have Facebook, or equivalent, sites where students with the same topic can gather, how can we avoid the study of *apples* being smothered, so to speak, in information? Someone will have a wonderful completed project detailing species of *trees* in the country or a history of *apple* species development, and students who come later can simply take what is already done, leaving them with little to discover for themselves. Well, in part, of course, this is the situation we are all in when we want to discover something new—we go to the Internet and find out what someone more expert has put there for us. While there is a danger of everything soon being too ready-prepared for students, there are a number of possible defenses. First, one can simply enlarge

the number of topics. Second, one can encourage students to see
the materials already available as one set among many potential
sources of knowledge they can use in building their personal portfolios. Third, one can expect past portfolios to support new ones
pushing further and further with topics, so that over time we may
expect many students to develop even greater expertise. Fourth,
for some of the less able students these prior portfolios on their
topic can help bootstrap their learning and help them discover
what aspects of the topic they most want to pursue; seeing knowledge organized by a number of other students may prove much
less intimidating than exploring the kinds of professional layouts
and finished forms we see in textbooks and online today. But there
are problems remaining, perhaps balanced by opportunities—so
while a finished portfolio might be intimidating to some younger
students, for others it might serve as an inspiration and stimulus.
So, yes, the Internet creates problems, but not, I think, insuper-
able ones.

Objection 10. You cite in favor of your proposal William H.
    Kilpatrick's Project Method, R. S. Peters's and Paul Hirst's
    justification for learning in depth, and Howard Gardner's
    ideas in *The Disciplined Mind,* but they all argue for quite
    different ideas of learning in depth.
The vice-principal at a Multiple Intelligences school for a number of years.
He gives regular workshops on MI theory and practice, and is completing
an Ed.D. degree and writing a thesis on implementing MI in regular school
settings.

The opening justification for this scheme mentions prominent scholars who have long argued that being educated meant
knowing something in depth as well as the usual "breadth" curriculum. But none of them even remotely suggested that learning in depth means what you have proposed. You mention R. S.
Peters and Paul Hirst, who applied modern philosophical analysis
to educational concepts. They didn't lay out a program for satisfying the depth criterion, because they thought that specifying

what "depth" meant in any area of knowledge was something that had to be worked out by disciplinary specialists. I'm sure they wouldn't accept your proposal as satisfying their sense of the depth criterion. They had in mind a (breadth) curriculum made up of a set of forms of knowledge, or fields derived from them. There were some, but not really significant, differences among them about what those forms of knowledge were—most included things like mathematics/logic, physical sciences, moral/religious thinking, interpersonal sensitivities, literature/fine arts, and historical understanding. Their notion of the breadth criterion was that students should gain some significant knowledge in each of the forms of knowledge, but their notion of the depth criterion was that students would learn one or more of these basic forms of knowledge in more detail. What constituted "depth," then, was not something for them to decide. Rather disciplinary experts would specify what degree of understanding of chemistry, say, or geography constituted understanding the subject in depth.

So, in the minds of the philosophers who have argued for learning in depth as a necessary criterion for any sensible notion of education, your proposal is rather eccentric. They meant that students should become well versed in history or chemistry, not that they should learn as much as anyone on earth about *apples* or *birds.*

Gardner's support for learning in depth leads to quite different programs from the idea you are suggesting. He details three powerful topics—Darwin's theory of evolution, Mozart's *The Marriage of Figaro,* and the Nazi Holocaust—and shows how a disciplined understanding of these, or other rich and complex topics like them, can have a transforming effect on people's minds, and how that transforming effect is properly what we mean by education. In contrast, your proposal is just an attenuated, serendipitous focus on topics with no resonance. Learning about *birds* in depth, in the sense you are suggesting, only gives you someone full of knowledge about birds: it does nothing to guarantee an educated person who understands important features of the human condition, with an appreciation of the importance of the old trinity of the good, the true, and the beautiful. Gardner's book looks in detail at how one can develop a disciplined mind, rather than let haphazard chance take the student where he or she wills in exploring a topic.

Gardner's book deals with learning in depth in a way that raises the most fundamental questions about our lives and civilization; it addresses issues that are both timelessly important to all people and also urgent political issues. Your proposal is trivial in comparison.

You also referred earlier to the Project Method of Kilpatrick and the current developments of that work by Katz and Chard. It should be pointed out that for Kilpatrick the project was an instrument of engaging students in important social learning and what he called "wholehearted purposeful activity." He saw it as a key teaching methodology supporting progressivism, and supporting John Dewey's calls for students to be actively involved in their own learning, breaking away from the dull knowledge-accumulating style of traditional education that imposed passivity on students. Both Kilpatrick and more recent Project Method proponents try to get students to work together on practical projects to solve some problem and involve them in important social learning. It developed from methods of training student-architects to solve practical problems in sixteenth-century Italy (Knoll 1995). Your proposal seems almost to be going backward, leaving students mainly working by themselves and having no social aims. Yours seems to focus only on individuals' minds, with little attention to the rich social and cultural environments that provide minds with their nurturance and enable moral democratic social activity to enrich our lives. It is like a throwback that ignores all the educational achievements of progressivism.

Response to: You cite in favor of your proposal William H. Kilpatrick's Project Method, R. S. Peters's and Paul Hirst's justification for learning in depth, and Howard Gardner's ideas in The Disciplined Mind, *but they all argue for quite different ideas of learning in depth.*

True, and, of course, it's not as though my proposal is being made in some kind of competition with those other proposals. I'm not sure what R. S. Peters or Paul Hirst would make of LiD. I read and reread much of their work looking for their proposals for achieving the kind of depth study they proposed as necessary for adequate education, but couldn't find anything. As the vice-principal noted, they left the job of filling out what would be required to content area specialists. Their sense of "depth" also seemed to be the kind of specialized study that used to be common in British grammar schools or "public" schools decades ago and that occurs in some high schools or at least in colleges and universities today. That is, Peters and Hirst were not making some innovative proposal for how to achieve learning in depth so much as indicating the importance of achieving some form of depth learning as a criterion for education. That my proposal is not what they had in mind, then, doesn't disturb me. The reason I mentioned them was because they do argue for the educational necessity of "depth," and while they did not point to what I am proposing, the richness and elaborateness of exploration that will likely occur in the Learning in Depth project is very much in the spirit of their criterion. I suspect they would approve of this project at least as a kind of supplement to what they meant by their depth criterion.

I have cited Howard Gardner's arguments in favor of learning in depth because I think they are good ones, and because I think they add important support to an educational aim we generally share, even though his book deals with much larger issues than this one. My book, indeed, proposes a much more attenuated proposal than does his, and mine touches on virtually none of the important themes that he explores. But, even so, I think it is worth considering whether this relatively attenuated and trivial proposal might not also contribute something significant, be more practicable, and perhaps even be more likely to achieve the kind of deeper understanding for which we are aiming.

What this book offers most importantly is a simple and practical program that can be relatively easily implemented. This proposal doesn't rely on some substantial change in teachers' professional training, nor in the structure of schooling, nor does it require changes to the curriculum beyond this addition, nor virtuoso teaching, nor any of the other conditions that most educational proposals for significant changes require. That is, this proposal could be implemented alongside today's typical curriculum and also alongside a curriculum that has been changed in the ways Gardner recommends.

And the vice-principal is right about the Project Method too. While it aims for rich learning with clear social and moral purposes, it is worth considering whether my more attenuated proposal might not lead to similar ends. Certainly there are obvious differences between project work and what I am proposing, many of the differences being along the lines he has pointed out. (Here is a description of the Project Method: "an educational enterprise in which children solve a practical problem over a period of several days or weeks. It may involve building a rocket, designing a playground, or publishing a class newspaper. The projects may be suggested by the teacher, but they are planned and executed as far as possible by the students themselves, individually or in groups. Project work focuses on applying, not imparting, specific knowledge or skills, and on improving student involvement and motivation in order to foster independent thinking, self-confidence, and social responsibility." Taken gratefully from the *Education Encyclopedia*—at http://education.stateuniversity.com/pages/2337/Project-Method.html. What this description plays down is Kilpatrick's focus on purposeful activity by students working in common to a common purpose: a consciously aimed at training for democratic citizenship.) None of the proposals for projects that I have seen even considers projects focusing on a single topic for all the years of schooling. What projects have in common with my proposal is the recognition that focused learning in greater depth has educational values beyond simply accumulating inert knowledge. Besides that there are probably more differences than similarities.

I'm not sure, by the way, that the Learning in Depth project will involve students in quite the lonely and unsociable activity the vice-principal suggest. Certainly some democratic social life with its requisite virtues is not part of the explicit aim of this project. But the students will be in constant contact with their teachers; they will be encouraged to have contact with others pursuing the same topic or other topics with which connections might be made. They will also be encouraged to talk to parents, relations, family friends, the guy across the hall, experts, and others, in the process of building their portfolios. Also I expect that all kinds of networks will develop quite quickly around particular topics. I imagine Web sites devoted to each topic that would attract students from around the area or country or world who might share a topic. Imagine the *apple* sites, and how the students themselves might elaborate it, organize joint projects across cultures, etc. One teacher said that she saw the project offering fantastic possibilities for "distributed learning." This isn't, then, quite the solitary enterprise envisioned by setting it in contrast to the sociability aimed for in the Project Method. Indeed, one of the unexpected features of the first "pirate" pilot programs, as one teacher calls them, was her constantly seeing children bringing in books or magazines or pictures for their friends because they had seen something about *cats* or *ants* or whatever that might be useful for the friend's portfolio.

I am in danger of making virtues of my deficiencies perhaps, making this Learning in Depth project's rather stark simplicity—compared to those projects the vice-principal cites to denigrate mine—seem as though what it lacks might be in its favor. But I confess I do think that there is a virtue in the starkness and apparent simplicity of this proposal. To adequately defend this claim would have to take us into philosophical depths beyond this book, and beyond me, but let me sketch the argument I think is relevant here. The proposals for project work or for depth learning that are tied in with progressivist theories of education tend to see the problem of failures to learn adequately in school as social or psychological issues to be resolved by improved forms of pedagogy or provision of better resources. Now clearly there is something in this. But I think the nature of knowledge and the nature of the mind are such that accumulating knowledge in depth about even so apparently insignificant a topic as *apples* can yield some of the benefits that Peters and Hirst want, and that Gardner's book describes, and that the Project Method aims for.

An iconic feature of progressivism is a deep suspicion of learning a lot of content because this can so easily look like "rote learning" or "accumulating inert knowledge." This was the "traditionalist" sin that progressivism was going to save us from by making all learning relevant to students' experience and meaningful in their everyday active lives. What has tended to get lost in all this is recognition that, mostly, minds just don't leave knowledge "inert." The belief that underlies Learning in Depth is that knowledge itself, as it is accumulated in unforced conditions, will grow and develop and enrich experience in ways we would all agree are of educational value. The "unforced conditions" of the LiD project are in contrast to the kind of "formal learning" that Dewey (1966, p. 9) derided as a cause of so much of students' alienation from the content of the school curriculum. Accumulating increasingly complex knowledge will usually generate its own tool kits for making increasingly sophisticated sense of that knowledge.

Now that may all seem rather arcane, and it is certainly too condensed, but I will return to elaborate on what I mean in Appendix A. What I want to do here is acknowledge that some of the oddities of this proposed project, in the context of current educational orthodoxies, don't mean that there are not alternative and sensible ideas supporting it.

Even though the topics I am proposing may seem trivial compared with evolution, Mozart, and the Holocaust, each topic can lead to some profound understanding, which can also transfer widely to other topics. In the next chapter I will be looking at the criteria that will determine what will serve as suitable topics. One criterion is that the topics can lead to important features of cultural life and also can engage the emotions and imaginations of students. I tend to think that this criterion excludes little, though, for various pragmatic reasons, we will find that certain topics might prove clearly better and some will be clearly problematic and should be excluded.

What is in danger of becoming a mantra for this project—everything is interesting, if only one learns enough about it—points at the way in which these seemingly trivial topics all unfold into the depths of our history, culture, and experience. So, again, this is indeed a limited idea, and the topics may appear on the face of it simple, but I think the result for most students will be transformative.

Objection 11. The reality of schooling is increasing pressure for greater success at meeting state-mandated standards. To this urgent requirement on schools, this proposal contributes nothing. It offers only a whimsical and inefficient form of teaching, and will not be taken seriously by anyone in authority in education, especially as it is lacking data to show that the scheme actually works or could work in schools.
A professor of education serving as research advisor to the school board. She has a Ph.D. in curriculum and instruction, and conducts research into methods of assessment. She has published three widely used books on student assessment and many articles comparing the effectiveness of different methods of instruction.

We are in a world where the reality of schooling is state-mandated standards and exams, and this proposal is just way off in the clouds as far as any administrator is concerned, or any teacher whose daily worry is preparing kids to meet those standards and pass those exams. Any innovation will be looked at in terms of whether it will contribute to this demand on schools or not. This will clearly not contribute. Three related reasons why it will fail come to mind.

First, this project looks like the rightly criticized "topic" approach to teaching early reading, in which quite different stories are brought together under topics like "horses" or "other countries." The stories are unified only by a name, not by an underlying domain of reality or genre, and so the whole exercise loses any real meaning. I see this depth scheme would go the same way—it might be that kids would look at all kinds of disciplines and approaches focused on "apples," but that's an arbitrary and spurious pulling together of subject matter that can be more efficiently studied in their usual subject areas. And I suspect that this LiD program will quickly come to resemble ordinary schooling, and not necessarily the best kind of ordinary schooling.

Second, I worry most about the simple inefficiency of this as an instructional method. There have been many studies of project-based teaching, and they have shown it to use school time far less productively than straightforward teaching of subject matter. I'm thinking of Jeanne Chall's book *The Academic Achievement Challenge: What Really Works in the Classroom?* (2002). What doesn't work is unproductive use of classroom time, and such project-focused class activities work even less well with disadvantaged students. So introducing such a program would doubly disadvantage such students when our greatest challenge is to narrow the achievement gap between them and better performing kids.

And third, I don't see at all how we can follow this depth plan and still meet our mandated state standards. To get over that hump, this project will need to persuade state legislatures that are currently moving toward more, not less, grade-by-grade content specificity, and I can't see them being persuaded. And, most simply, there just isn't any data that it will work or can work, as my colleague already pointed out.

Response to: The reality of schooling is increasing pressure for greater success at meeting state-mandated standards. To this urgent requirement on schools, this proposal contributes nothing. It offers only a whimsical and inefficient form of teaching, and will not be taken seriously by anyone in authority in education, especially as it is lacking data to show that the scheme actually works or could work in schools.

I think some part of the professor's objection is caused by a misunderstanding about how the program is intended to work. In her comment about this being an inefficient form of teaching, she seems to imagine the students doing their work in a LiD class. But this project is designed to happen largely outside regular class time. For the first three years the students will likely need the most teacher support, and teachers will meet with students individually or in small groups to discuss their portfolios and make suggestions for further study, and so on, as I've described above. That might happen in the regular classroom, but it could happen in the school library or some other place in the school that might be convenient. The teachers will not be instructing students about *apples* or *birds* or *the circus* in a class setting, or indeed at all. There may be some time during the day in those early years when students might work at their desks on their projects or in the library, but LiD is not competing for class time with other subjects. It is an add-on. But it is an add-on that is intended to be worked on increasingly outside the school, much as students might spend time with a hobby or a collection. Students will be allotted some brief occasions at school for consultation with the teacher about the project, for suggestions or questions about what they might do next, for appreciation and encouragement, and so on. They may also work on their topics if they have finished some other work early and the teacher lets them pursue their topic, and they might use the school library at various times to develop their portfolios. But they will not be "inefficiently" taught about their topics.

I should also indicate how LiD in practice is not likely to be as cut off from regular classroom activities as I have maybe so far suggested. Apart from the skills developed in the LiD project transferring to students' learning in the regular curriculum, teachers can use the knowledge, understanding, and engagement students are acquiring in their LiD studies for other learning. The following is an example of a teacher currently supervising a LiD program, even though integrating LiD with the regular curriculum work may not usually be as deliberate as this:

We've integrated LiD with the curriculum. For example, our current
math strand is data management, so we have the kids create graphs
or Venn diagrams based on the data in their LiD topics. Later when
we do procedural writing, instead of describing how to brush one's
teeth (not a topic with huge student engagement!) the rabbit expert
can describe how to trim a rabbit's toenails, and the other experts can
describe something related to their topics. (Dale Hubert, Ontario,
Canada)

Other teachers have indicated how they quickly began to routinely draw on students' growing expertise while teaching basic
curriculum units. When working on a unit concerning Peru,
for example, one teacher said it just seemed natural to ask if the
apples expert could tell them something about apple production
in Peru, or the railways expert could tell them something about
railways in the country, and, if not, ask the students to find out
for next class, thereby adding something to the portfolio and also
to everyone's knowledge about Peru. Having the growing range of
expertise on twenty or thirty topics in the class enriches learning
about everything else.

The professor thinks that current realities unambiguously
doom the LiD project. I have two responses to this objection; the
first is to argue that there are good reasons to believe that students
engaged in LiD will be more likely to do well on such mandated
tests than students who do not experience the stimulation of the
program, and the second concerns "reality."

A central aim of the LiD program is to transform students' relationship to, and understanding of the nature of, knowledge. In the
process it will also involve each student in intensive and extensive exploration, classification, analysis, and experiments over the
years of its operation. That is, each year students will have to reas-
sess their portfolios, culling, adding, reorganizing, reclassifying,
and learning a range of cognitive skills that will be available for
other tasks and study of other curriculum areas, and these skills
predict greater not less success for these students. It seems to me
the far likelier outcome will be that these students will be much

better equipped to make sense of the material on which mandated tests will be based, and will be able to perform better.

But still there is "reality." First, I dispute the view that current realities of a test-driven regime will disadvantage LiD students, and, second, I want to make the trite observation that realities change. We have been living for a few years with an agenda of constraining and shaping teachers' activities by means of standards and testing. These have been imposed by governments in response to the belief that these instruments will bring about improvements in the educational attainments of our schools. What will be "the reality" if it becomes clear that the current testing procedures fail to produce the results that have been promised and that they have been designed to bring about—if it becomes clear that this is an inadequate solution because its designers failed to recognize the true cause of the problem of students' inadequate achievements? What if our new reality in five years is improved student test scores and students' increasing lack of interest in and engagement with the subjects in which they are scoring better, with a precipitous decline in students choosing to pursue, say, math and the sciences? (See Egan 2008 for an examination of this problem and current "solutions.") Either way, if "reality" includes a continuance of the current testing regime or whether it gives way to quite different practices, I see no reason to think LiD will not be a significant addition to students' education.

I'm not sure how one is to respond at this point to the dismissive assertion that there is no data to suggest the program does or can work. It is, after all, a twelve-year program: because there is no data about its results, we can't implement it, and if we can't implement it, there will be no data. This seems a bit Catch-22-ish. Well, that's too cute a response, of course. There are currently some pilot projects underway, but we need more in different school conditions. And, reasonably, people need reasons to consider setting up a pilot program, even if initially only for a year or so. But that is what this book is trying to provide—reasons that the LiD program is worth implementing. In the future, after this book—I hope—encourages many implementation programs, then we may be able to provide the "data" the professor requires now. Her requirement would, of course, have prevented every educational innovation in history from getting off the ground.

Conclusion

Well, I trust no one can claim this set of questions was chosen for being easy to answer. These are all potential criticisms that have occurred to me, or have been made by someone after a talk, and they are all reasonable objections that do need some response. I've provided a response to each in order to preserve the proposal in its original form. Some of the objections, however, do carry force. I can't equally easily reject them all. A number of strong objections seem to gather around the earliest years. How does one get a five-year-old who cannot read or write to begin a portfolio on *apples* or *trees?* I do think that, with imaginative teaching, this is quite possible (and we have put on our Web site at www.ierg.net/lid elaborate examples of how this may be done, taking as our first two examples *apples* and *money*). But it's not simply imaginative teaching that may be in short supply when teachers have so many other pressures on their days. I have tried to suggest ways we can get around the problems of time constraints, but, for those first years, there are limits to how well we can manage this without making an investment in increasing staffing or shifting priorities and time from other school activities.

The biggest time requirement posed by the proposal so far is for the period before students are able to read and write easily or work with some degree of independence. One compromise with the original proposal would be to begin the LiD project in grade 3.

If we start when students are seven or eight years old, the more problematic objections lose some of their force. The time constraints are relieved significantly if we do not need to have extra support in place for the first few years, though, of course, they don't disappear. By grade 3, though, it is easier to imagine that teachers might be able to manage the supervision required, if they are supported by older students, librarians, volunteer parents, or if priorities are changed to reduce time spent on some other program(s), and/or a small increase in pay is provided.

I'm not convinced that we couldn't get the project underway at kindergarten or grade 1, but I acknowledge that it will be a lot easier for many concerned if it officially starts in grade 3. This would have the further advantage that in the first two grades some deliberate preparation for the beginning of the portfolios can be taught. Certainly students can learn some of the basic skills they will need to successfully launch their portfolios. While these are skills—like reading and writing, classifying, etc.—that students in the first two grades would learn anyway, it should be easy to include a specific focus on the ways these skills would best enable them to make a successful beginning to their portfolios.

But yet, having said all that, I still think it would be better to start with grade 1, and some educators I have spoken with think it could quite successfully be begun in kindergarten. In the first week of the year in which it is begun the student will be allotted a topic. The beginnings of their exploration might simply involve talking with others about their own special topic, with which they are going to become very familiar. One large-scale implementation program currently underway included a set of three questions for the students to stimulate interest in the topic and set them off exploring. The students can ask parents, older students, and other people they meet what they can tell them about it, and how they might go about answering the questions. They can look at books, draw pictures, learn to write the word TREE/APPLE/TRAIN if they can't already write. Something of Sylvia Ashton-Warner's idea of "keywords" (1972) can leverage the topic as a motivator to reading and writing. (Ashton-Warner worked with Maori children in her native New Zealand, distressed that they seemed unable to learn to read and write with any efficiency by the methods commonly used in the British colonial school system. She talked with each child, locating what they felt most strongly about, and generated from each child's passions and hopes and fears a "key vocabulary," which she then used in literacy instruction. She had remarkable success, and her "keywords" method became widely, but not widely enough, used.) While the randomly assigned topics are not keywords in her sense, they can gather exactly that aura of a special area of knowledge that the students own, and will come to own in a unique way, during many years, and, indeed, to the end of their lives.

So the first two years of students beginning to explore their topics and make the first moves toward developing their portfolios may not need to impinge in a problematic way on administrative ingenuity or teachers' time or make other unsustainable demands on schools. If we treat the first two years as more informal, ensuring only that the students are constantly reminded of their topics and provided with something like a special physical portfolio to begin collecting whatever materials they can find about their topics, and in which they can keep their drawings and beginning attempts to write and classify what they are learning about it, that may be sufficient.

::::

Looking at a set of objections and trying to make responses to them maybe leaves us at this point with a sense of the project as a series of battles and struggles, fighting objections that may loom large in readers' minds. This has not been the frame of mind in which the project has developed so far, and so it may be worthwhile at this point to try to reassert quite briefly what the program is likely to contribute when conditions are even moderately favorable to it.

We have largely been looking at the problems of implementing this idea into a system in which nothing much like it has existed, and that has focused us on the difficulties and particularly on what seem the problems of getting the whole process started with young children who have no models of what the program leads to. So let me try to give a quick description of its possible benefits once in regular practice.

The LiD program is something new and additional that the school can offer to students' education. The program is relatively simple and straightforward and requires little in the way of additional resources. It provides a new way in which students can build knowledge, understanding, skills, and practices fundamental to effective learning, and this expanded capacity is available for all other schooling beyond immediate work in the program.

Students will first learn about something in depth, accumulating expertise on some topic to the point where they will develop genuine expertise. This deep acquaintance with one topic will also inevitably provide students with a growing understanding of the nature of knowledge in general, clarifying for them increasingly the difference between degrees of security of knowledge claims and of opinions. A possibly unexpected benefit of the program, but one that is an important aim, is that knowledge in depth will provide a stimulus for students' imaginations—our imaginations can work only with what we know; ignorance is the great enemy of imagination. Growing expertise in some area of knowledge will increase students' confidence as learners, and this benefit should also spread to their other learning in school. As portfolios grow, the students will have to reorganize a number of times the knowledge they have accumulated, and this will stimulate development of increasingly complex classifying and organizing skills, along with the associated skills to manage such reorganization on the Internet.

Mostly this book is about the benefit of this program to students, which is appropriate, but it also offers a number of benefits to teachers. Unlike most teaching/learning relationships, in this case after quite a short time the students will know more about their specific topic than do the teachers who will be helping them construct their portfolios. The teachers' skills will be deployed in guiding the students' further inquiries, but the teachers will also be exploring and discovering a wide range of knowledge along with their students. This constant exploration and discovery of new knowledge should be a frequent and pleasant intellectual stimulus to teachers. Teachers will also have the experience of constant interaction with enthusiastic learners, and the results of their explorations are not to be subjected to assessment and grading. These knowledgeable students will not keep their new skills confined to the LiD topic, but will bring them to all the regular classes of the daily curriculum. It is likely that this new and different form of student engagement with knowledge and the associated skills it will stimulate will enrich all teaching.

The program will likely have other effects that will influence the whole school, especially after a few years if all the students are pursuing topics of their own. It will transform the school from a place in which students are the novices who are gaining a general and rather superficial understanding of the range of human knowledge to a place that becomes additionally a center of expertise in a wide range of topics. If the program develops over a number of years, then it seems quite likely that it will transform the school in a number of both clear and subtle ways. Schools can display students' expertise in a variety of forms. Schools can schedule frequent presentations on topics to the whole school as students reach particular stages in their portfolio development, and students will become more expert in presenting their knowledge to others, with teachers' help. "Ask the expert" sessions may be scheduled, for other students, for parents, and via phone-in radio shows for the public at large. It is reasonable to expect that with expertise will come greater imagination, greater seriousness about learning, and greater enthusiasm for learning, and that these changes of attitude will influence the culture of schools. Wall displays of students' topics should provide an attractive central focus in the school.

Students of different ages in an area, in a region, and across the country, and even from around the world, can begin to make contact on the basis of their shared topic to create new forms of interaction centered on learning. The grade 10, grade 7, and grade 2 students who are building portfolios on *apples* can meet and work together, perhaps facilitated by a college student; they may build their own Web site, which can be linked with perhaps dozens of other students' Web sites about *apples;* there can be online discussions and presentations on the topic, and students of all ages can be engaged at their own level. That is, if this program begins to be implemented quite widely, we may see new structures and networks whereby schools encourage and promote learning.

Of course, this may seem like a somewhat optimistic fantasy that ignores the problems we have been wrestling with in this chapter. And I don't imagine those problems simply vanishing if we only put LiD into practice. But it is useful, I think, to dwell briefly on the intended benefits of the program after dealing so long with potential difficulties. No doubt implementing it will require some new challenges and some adjustments to the current routines of schooling. It does no good to try to suggest, as I may occasionally be in danger of suggesting, that this program can be slipped into current school systems without any effects other than those of students building more than usual knowledge about something. If the program works as I think it might, it will likely have some significant and perhaps unexpected ramifications throughout the school system, but I think they will be very largely beneficial.

The Nature of the Topics 4

Several of the objections to the program have helped to make it clear that proposing students learn any topic in depth is not enough. Some kinds of topics just don't seem to be able to do the job for us—they might allow a student to accumulate masses of knowledge, but if it is at much the same level, as would likely be the case with collecting baseball or cricket statistics, that won't do. We need topics that have the richness and complexity to sustain multidimensional exploration for a dozen years. My purpose for this chapter is to come up with a set of criteria that can help determine what will serve as suitable topics for students to study for twelve years, and also to come up with a list of suitable topics.

I'll begin with some topics that seem to me well able to do the job. That is, they will be topics that young students will find engaging, and that are sufficiently rich and complex to support the changing interests students will bring to them during their years in schooling. Then I'll look at a set of topics that might seem on their surface suitable, but, for one reason or another, are unlikely to do the job for us. From these two initial explorations I hope to begin establishing some clear criteria that can be used to guide us to many other topics that are suitable for extended and varied study. Then I'll simply try to generate in a few minutes a more or less random list of further topics and use them as tests of the criteria developed so far. My hope is that examining these more or less randomly chosen topics will help refine the criteria. I will conclude with both a list of criteria that will help anyone wishing to locate a set of topics for a class or school, and a preliminary list of topics.

The topics that are to be explored need to be complex, varied, and multidimensional—to allow for more than a decade of exploration as students go through the usual changes in interests over the years from about five to eighteen. It would appear that the topics we choose for students to satisfy the depth criterion must have breadth and depth criteria of their own, with an added criterion to do with their having multiple dimensions to keep growing minds and different minds engaged. So we already have three criteria to begin work on—*breadth, depth,* and what I'll call *participation.* Let's consider these three in a little more detail, and then later we can use them to explore specific topics to see how well the topics measure up, and also explore how the topics can help us refine these first three criteria.

1. The breadth criterion requires that the topic has to have a lot of multidisciplinary material implicit in it. So *apples* is an adequate topic according to this criterion because there is a lot of biological, historical, cultural, nutritional, economic, artistic, and so on, information about apples. That is, even if we were to treat apples as a topic for pure knowledge accumulation and classification, there is a lot of knowledge to accumulate and classify.

2. The depth criterion requires that students will have the possibility of increasingly detailed exploration. So the biology of apples and their history, and so on, can allow rich specificity that ramifies in many directions. As we explore in depth we come to recognize the "inside" of the topic—we know its limits and extremes; we know what there is to know, even if we haven't yet learned it all; we gain expertise. As our understanding becomes deeper, so our sense of the nature of knowledge becomes more

complex and subtle. Each topic will have to have the complexity to allow this.

3. The third criterion requires that the topics are amenable to exploration in multiple modalities. That is, the topics must yield something other than simply accumulations of knowledge in breadth and depth, and must offer opportunities for cultural and personal engagements. This further dimensional criterion may be seen as connecting the topic with our sense of self in some way. The depth criterion might be seen as an ally in this, but I think there is something further involved—the topic must have the potential for our emotions to become entangled with it. Not simply in the sense that we grow to love or hate it, but that we become a part of what we have learned so much about and it becomes a part of us. The topic will invade our thinking. In the odd way the mind engages with knowledge in depth, it isn't simply that we learn about something that remains external to us, but that—and it is appropriate to repeat the phrase for something that is evident in many people's experience though we have no precise language to capture it—the topic becomes a part of us; we participate in it.

This language of subtle understanding of the "inside" of a topic, and its ramifying complexities, and its transforming in some degree our very sense of ourselves, may appear not only vague but, even if it is reluctantly permitted due to the difficulty of describing such experiences, may seem relevant only to the most refined scholarly attainments among the best and brightest scholars. It may seem hopelessly out of place referring to those kids from impoverished backgrounds who have difficulty learning basic literacy. But, yes, I do mean it to refer to those kids, because I think they are the ones we most shortchange in schools at the moment, and this is one possible way of giving them access to some aspects of the education of which they are currently largely deprived.

So we need to choose topics such that students can, as it were, extensively roam their wide surface, they must have sufficient specificity so that students can plumb down beneath the surface to significant depths of understanding, and they must have dimensions of cultural richness, ensuring that they ramify into our lives and emotions and imaginations.

Let us look at some topics, beginning with those rather casually listed at the beginning of the book, and see how well they stack up against these three criteria. The other purpose for examining some topics in a little more detail is to see whether some further criteria for selection or rejection of topics emerge. At the beginning of chapter 2, I suggested *apples, the wheel, mollusks, railways, leaves, ships, the circus, spices,* and *dust.* Let me begin with the last of these: it was suggested slightly mischievously, as a topic that might seem hopelessly inadequate for a five-year-old to become interested in and then study for a further decade or so.

Dust

How does *dust* stack up against our three criteria? Is there sufficient "surface" knowledge to explore for a long time? At first sight this doesn't seem altogether promising; I mean, dust is just that gray stuff we spend time wiping away constantly. But what is dust made of? Well, that's where it begins to get interesting. In a typical room, maybe 60 percent of it is decayed human skin, which leads us into a lot of biology. The biology continues with an exploration of the next largest component of common dust accumulations: those creatures that live off the decayed skin, such as dust mites. There's much to learn about these lovely characters—their life cycle, their implication in human diseases, and their own dead bodies adding to the dust they live with. Some of the dust in the normal dwelling comes from minute fibers of clothing, especially from cottons. Jeans are major contributors. So just dealing with the dust in an average room provides a significant amount of knowledge, even before we start looking at various forms of environmental dust, exploding dust, dust in space, and so on.

How many grains of dust are in the average classroom? How could we begin to calculate that? One can build a sense of wonder about dust's ubiquity. What is it doing floating in the air of every room? What vast dramas of varied life forms are going on unseen in the air we breath, rich in pollens, viruses, and bacteria, and rich too—the engaging "Yuck!" factor—in the feces of flies and other insects? Unseen, but like galaxies strewn with stars, thronged with creatures living and dying and fighting each other in cosmic battles before our eyes, but mostly unrecognized. Except that the student who is given dust as a topic will begin to see that what others take for granted is full of astonishing drama and wonder.

Let's briefly imagine how a student might build a portfolio on *dust*. In the first year the student—let's call him Nathan—who has received *dust* as his topic learns that in a typical house about a thousand dust particles settle on each square centimeter (with a drawing of how big that is) every hour of the day. Where is it coming from? His teacher tells him that a lot of this is from human skin, and that we shed the whole outer layer of our skin every day or two, which comes off at the rate of about 7 million flakes of skin each minute (with some indications of how many this is). Yuck! Nathan is beginning to understand why there is so much dust around. And that's only the skin—there's much more in dust, he begins to discover. He begins a list of all the things that he discovers make up the dust in his classroom, including flakes from clothing, pollens from plants, fly poop—yuck again!—and much else. He has magnified pictures of dust mites, and a small plastic pouch of dust stapled into his portfolio file, with a list of its content attached.

As he moves on to grade 2, he will continue to meet with his teacher regularly to discuss ideas about dust and what to explore next. His portfolio is already bulging with further drawings and photographs of dust mites and other miniature creatures found in dust, pages of varied facts, plastic containers with kinds of dust, lists of places where dust storms are common, pictures of dust clouds in space and on earth from space, a note of how "pixie dust" is used in *Peter Pan* to help people to fly, and on and on.

As he moves into his middle school years, he can begin to search out further material on the Internet, gathering information, and

constructing, with teachers' help, categories to classify and reorganize his accumulating store of knowledge. He begins to add
videos of atmospheric dust storms, dust in space, and so on, discovering whole new forms of dust to explore.

For the next few years the major growth in Nathan's portfolio
comes from online developments, though experiential exploration continues to be significant. For nearly a year Nathan might
explore "records," such as the largest accumulations of dust and
the most dust-free environments, and also explore explosive dust,
colorful dust, uses of dust particles in space exploration, gold dust,
underwater dust, dust in literature, Dust Bowl conditions, dust in
songs, and so on. His own interests are increasingly the driver in
these explorations, and teachers should feel it appropriate to encourage quite quirky pathways of inquiry, like underwater dust or
the health problems associated with dust mites.

As he moves through high school years, Nathan increasingly realizes the wonder of dust, which is everywhere, all over the earth,
and through the stars, and, even in the cleanest conditions, thousands of dust grains are in every cubic inch of air. If his family is
attentive to his growing expertise, Nathan may receive occasional
gifts—the uncle returning from Australia with a small sample of
gold dust, the grandfather's birthday gift of a picture book about
Dust Bowl experiences, the parents' present of a microscope, etc.

The subject of Nathan's inquiries is in size about half way between a subatomic particle and the planet he lives on. He will become increasingly aware as his portfolio develops of the processes
of life and of social and historical conditions that are interwoven
with his topic. Well, I will not keep inventing such quick scenarios, but I hope it is clear how even so unlikely a topic "exfoliates"
to reveal rich dimensions for exploration.

The second criterion suggests that these explorations of dust in
breadth can also lead to further explorations in depth. From classifying forms of dust, beginning with the generally accepted defi-
nition of tiny solid particles of less than five hundred micrometers
in diameter, we can take any of the breadth topics and plunge

down into greater and greater detail. The richness of knowledge about a wide range of such topics can fill years of exploration in detail—dust in space offers many topics for detailed exploration, such as in comets' tails streaming out in those multimillion-mile-long shining processions of charged particles; dust in human habitation offers many topics to explore in great detail, as do environmental forms of dust.

Did you know that wind storms that rip across China's Taklimakan desert suck up hundreds of thousands of tons of dust, which are then caught in currents, rise high into the atmosphere, and are carried around the world in less than two weeks? As winds push against the Tibetan plateau the dust is carried up to five thousand meters. Some of the dust falls in the U.S. Pacific Northwest, some in the Atlantic, some in the Balkans. This dust, along with other massive clouds of similar particles, contributes to global cooling by reflecting sunlight. The mineral-rich dust helps nourish waters off the north Pacific, depositing iron that feeds phytoplankton, the microscopic marine plants that are an essential and basic link in the oceans' food chain.

And there are endless other details one can pursue. Did you know that "khaki" is the Urdu word for dust? One of the first large-scale cases of camouflage was achieved by the British army in their nineteenth-century invasion of Afghanistan. They found that washing their white uniforms in the ubiquitous red/brown dust provided them with greater safety, thus bringing the word "khaki" into English for the color their uniforms became after washing.

All very well, but how are we to get emotional about dust? What can make someone feel some connection with this topic at a personal level? Partly the affective connection to an area of knowledge will come willy-nilly as one simply learns more and more, in breadth and depth. It becomes one's own knowledge; one begins to get inside it and, as it were, feel at home within it. But, in addition to this, we will want to find some dimensions of dust that have a richer cultural resonance. The ancient Hebrew tradition makes resonantly clear that we should always remember that we are made from dust and unto dust we shall return. (A view given a further dimension in our growing understanding of the history of the cosmos. Stars explode, streaming particles through the galaxy. Dust clouds congeal from these particles, are drawn together by gravity, and plummet into massive agglomerations that become stars and planets, which go through chemical turmoil, which, in turn, produces us. We are made from stars and the dust they explode into—as Carl Sagan so vividly expressed it in his *Cosmos* TV series some decades ago.) Poets and writers commonly use dust as a metaphor for sterility and nothingness—"A handful of dust," "dust upon a sleeve," etc. To the student who gets dust as a topic, it will always seem like a handful of wonder, more like Peter Pan's pixie dust.

Well, that's my attempt to suggest how an initially unlikely looking topic can slip through the criteria established so far. I have to admit that if two children are sitting next to one another on the day they receive their topics and one gets *the circus* and the other gets *dust*, it's hard not to feel the *dust* kid is going to need some extra support! But, again, one of the things this project is to teach is that everything is interesting, if only you learn enough about it.

Apples

I think this topic has already been shown to be suitable from the discussions of it as an example earlier. The ease with which it satisfies all the criteria points again to the appropriateness of topics from the natural world for this project. In some ways this is an ideal topic, in that it has opportunities for significant classification, a natural history, and is tied in with human cultural history in endless ways. This readiness of natural world topics to satisfy the criteria does incline me to think that perhaps we might use all natural world topics for the LiD program. Some of my colleagues are not at all convinced of this, so let us consider a wide variety of topics for now.

The Wheel

At first glance, this looks like a likely topic. The invention of the wheel was clearly of profound importance in human cultural history, even though some quite sophisticated cultures existed for centuries without it. There have been many kinds of wheel, allowing significant classifying, even though the kinds of wheel might seem to be fewer in variety than kinds of dust. The basic technology of the wheel is quite simple to grasp, and there are many sophisticated uses of the wheel in human technology. The array of uses found for wheels in our lives is enormous: keeping time in watches, rapid transportation, computer hard drives, fans, moving heavy furniture, skateboards and other recreational vehicles, etc ; and, implicit in much of the above, there is a rich and complex history of the wheel that can be explored. That is, it would seem that the first criterion can easily be satisfied.

But how about the second? Can we stop at many points in our exploration across the plain of knowledge about the wheel and plunge down into great detail about aspects of it? Is "the wheel in clockwork," say, sufficiently varied to allow deep exploration? Is the knowledge rich and varied? Is the massive ingenuity of ratcheted, notched, transmission, balance, winding, etc., wheels sufficient, and sufficiently variable, to provide the kind of deep engagement required, and are there enough similar aspects of the topic? I'm not sure. This criterion is less easy to satisfy with regard to the wheel than with, say, dust, which reflects something of the difference between the natural world and that of technology.

The third criterion is, at first look, more easily or fully satisfied than the second. Contemplation of the wheel leads to reflections on human ingenuity. There was nothing in nature to suggest the wheel to people—nature gets on happily without wheels—though I gather there is some minute marine organism that has some kind of circular structure it uses for propulsion. But it certainly isn't one of those systems developed and wildly proliferated in the natural world as it is has in the world of technology. And it has transformed human lives immeasurably. We may think first of its almost universal use, in varied forms, in our massive and complex transportation systems, and how our species has developed into its current societies as a result of the wheel. It is an incidental but sustaining part of our lives, and also our arts and, of course, our sciences.

So it looks as though the student who is given the wheel as a topic will be able to learn in depth. What this topic raises, however, is whether the natural world offers topics of greater richness of study than our technology.

Mollusks

Well, the variety of mollusks exceeds those of apples by more than tenfold, and the variety even extends to spelling, as the British spelling is "molluscs." The array of mollusks varies from tiny snails and clams to squid and octopuses, and they inhabit nearly all marine environments, though most species prefer intertidal areas, and a few species, like snails and slugs live on land. They are a vital part of the ecological system, interacting with humans in almost as many ways as there are varieties of mollusk.

All three criteria seem easily satisfied by what may seem to some not the most exciting of topics—though I think you may be confident it will appear so by grade 12 to every student to whom it is allotted. (Jean Piaget started his career as a zoologist writing a paper on mollusks, published when he was aged fifteen, and completed his doctoral thesis on the topic at twenty-two.) This reinforces further the easy way in which topics in nature fulfill the criteria suggested so far.

Railways

Many of our topics have a history that goes back through the ages; the wheel disappears into human prehistory, represented in crude illustrations about 5,500 years ago, and wheels were in use maybe for a couple of millennia before that. But railways are relatively modern, certainly in the sense the term is generally understood today. In ancient Greece there is evidence of quite sophisticated systems for transporting boats across the Isthmus of Corinth made of parallel grooves etched in limestone. That Diolkos wagonway was in use for well over a thousand years. The wagons were pushed by slaves, and later horse-drawn carriages were kept on track in a similar way. But the "iron horse" that became the transportation backbone of developing industrial societies is an invention largely of the nineteenth century. The first "intercity" line was built in 1830 between Manchester and Liverpool in northwest England. In 1869 the symbolic last spike was driven into the rail line across the United States. There is no shortage of historical material.

The first criterion is readily satisfied by the complexity and variety of the railway systems of the world. The railroad tracks and points, the signaling systems, the rolling stock, the bridges and tunnels and their development. The second criterion similarly is easily satisfied. At any point one might branch into close detailed study of tunneling or bridge building, fashions of dress for railway travel in the nineteenth century, the vast and still astonishing Indian railway system, which remains the world's largest employer, the battles over track width or gauge, railway disasters, record-breaking runs, private railways, and on and on. The third criterion is also easy to satisfy. The railway has often been declared to be the most satisfying and romantic of all forms of transport. Even today, in the age of much faster airplanes, many will take a train, if at all possible. Given the new high-speed trains, especially throughout Europe and Japan, their ease and comfort continue to make them feel like a humane form of moving rapidly from one place to another. Novels and movies frequently take advantage of the lure of railways to suggest their romance both in terms of the ways our lives interact with them, and in their power and reliability.

Heroic stories abound connected with building railroads, from John Henry, the steel-driving man, to Casey Jones, and all those ghost trains. Trains also seem a favorite location for adventures, of heroic patience in the face of delays, or of scrambled timetables. One of my grandfather's favorite stories was about the time he had boarded a train in Poona station in India, during the later years of the British Raj. A florid Englishman got on, inspecting his ticket, and standing in consternation for a moment, looked down at the elegant Sikh gentleman in his seat. The Englishman said, a little outraged, "I say. You are sitting in my seat." The Sikh gentleman stood and took the ticket, examined it for a moment and replied cheerfully, "You are exceedingly correct, sir. But," sitting down again, "this is yesterday's train."

Leaves

This is a clear winner, in that it shares the qualities we have seen in most of the other topics about the natural world. It is both constrained on the one hand and also allows for great variety on the other. *Leaves* leads to a rich array of possibilities for classifying that are aesthetic as well as technical, that are richly tied into human cultures and imaginations through our association with plants of all kinds. Children can begin with collecting and classifying leaves, focusing first on the many local shapes and kinds. They can be led gradually into wondering why most leaves are thin and flat, and what purposes they perform for plants, and why they commonly change color in the fall. Collections of pressed leaves can add photographs of rare and strange varieties—including a section on "leaf records" (biggest, smallest, most leaf-fertile plant, thinnest, oldest known, most edible, most poisonous, etc.). Stories, poems, and pictures that draw attention to the beauty of many leaves and the places of leaves in the imagination of humankind can add human dimensions to a portfolio—as can the effects of the shade provided by leaves on human lives and buildings. This topic, like many in the natural world, is common and taken for granted but is potentially an object of fascination as knowledge grows about it, and is a topic that winds endlessly through human cultures. If *leaves*, then we can also include *flowers*, *berries*, *seeds*, and *roots*.

Ships

It looks like we should be able to add a series of topics connected with the technology of transportation. The only difficulty would seem to be choosing items that are sufficiently varied, have sufficient richness of material, and are sufficiently entangled with human history, hopes, dreams, emotions, and imagination. *Ships*, from earliest days to the present, are a topic that is able to satisfy all of our criteria quite easily. If *ships*, then we can perhaps also include *cars, airplanes,* and *bicycles.*

Cars as a topic is similar to *trains* in terms of lore and resonance. The stories of increasing speed attained in such vehicles, and the explicit drive for speed records, provides some drama, some need for classification and accumulations of statistics. *Airplanes* and *bicycles* are rather similar to *cars*, in that there is an adequate amount of variety and there is interesting historical material in people's earlier attempts to fly or to travel more quickly on land after the wheel's invention, and it is hard to think of an invention that has gained so much in transportational efficiency for so relatively small an outlay of energy as the bicycle.

The Circus

There have been many different kinds of circuses in history, including the traditional modern circus of clowns, trained animals, and acrobats; the ancient-world chariot races, staged battles, jugglers, and trained animals; ancient Chinese acrobatic displays; and the modern Cirque du Soleil involving a general storyline, music, and acrobatic performances. So, there is no shortage of variety in terms of the acrobatic acts, the animal performances, and the history of the different styles of circus. Circuses have appeared around the world, performing generally an entertaining role, tied in with regional characteristics and sometimes with regional politics.

The first criterion is fairly well satisfied. The second criterion is perhaps a little less easily satisfied. Though maybe those who specialize in, say, horse training, tightrope walking, or trapeze acts would disagree and argue that there are many areas for rich detailed study within the overall topic. I'm not sure how much we know with regard to, say, the ancient Chinese circus. Certainly there is a lot of material for detailed study of the ancient Roman circus. So, yes, maybe criterion two is satisfied.

The third criterion is more easily satisfied as the circus has always tried to confect magic out of sweat and training, and usually succeeded. Children who experience the circus early in their lives tend to carry a hint of its magic into adulthood. But the circus also can have deeper contacts with us. The appearance of the circus in so many books and movies suggests engagements with our emotions and imaginations that push beyond the surface entertainment. In Peter Carey's futuristic, or rather parallel, world, *The Unusual Life of Tristan Smith*, the circus (Sirkus) combines religious and social manipulation as well as "traditional" entertainment. It captures vividly how the circus, in a secular age, could quite easily shift from an aesthetic magic of daring performance to also touching on spiritual themes. One may see occasional hints of this in Cirque du Soleil's imprecise but engaging storylines, embedded in a surrounding and entrancing world of strange music and magical performance. Related topics might include the *Olympic games, winter sports,* and *fairs.*

Spices

This again is an easy winner. There are many spices, but a limited set. There is a richness of detail to be explored. The history of human discovery, cultivation, and attempts to acquire spices for dinner tables includes the European voyages of discovery, the clash of trading empires, and so on. While this topic does threaten to have too much content, it seems to me a solid topic for a rich portfolio. A colleague suggested that *salt* might also be used as a topic by itself.

: : :

Now I will look at a few topics that I had initially thought would be suitable, but with reflection seem problematic in one way or another. Examining these should add to the criteria we can use in selecting topics.

The Rings of Saturn

There is certainly quite a lot of knowledge about this topic now, our knowledge is growing quickly, and it has an immediate attractiveness. But this one might fall at the first criterion, and lead us to adding a rider to it. The problem, at least on the face of it, is that the knowledge that is indeed extensive is all rather technical. While the five-year-old might start classifying kinds of dust, and exploring some features of dust in an engaging way—more about which in the next chapter—it is hard to see that there is a lot of easily accessible knowledge about the rings of Saturn for the young child. I think, then, we need to refine our criteria to exclude topics to which initial access requires too much technical knowledge. A pity, as I was looking forward to including W. G. Sebald's *The Rings of Saturn* as one of the extensions of the topic into the self. So this leads us to a further criterion to apply to our choice of topics: *that they not initially be too technical.*

The initial access to topics is tied in with the potential difficulties of the first year or so. Some topics might seem perfectly suitable in general, but there may not be sufficient local resources for a child to make much headway into the topic. A colleague from Romania suggested that a topic like *fish* might be fine for a child in England, surrounded by water and easy access to a variety of fish and information about fish, but a child in Romania would be in a quite different situation. Now this isn't the only kind of reason why in some localities children might have difficulty finding resources to adequately get their portfolio going. So we have another criterion—*there must be sufficient resource materials for children in any locality to begin building an adequate portfolio.*

But maybe we might extend the rings of Saturn topic to *the solar system.* There is a lot more and more diverse knowledge available about it, and significant time might be spent discovering interesting knowledge about its quite diverse components. Young students might learn the dramatic story of its formation, and then the hugely diverse bits that currently make up *the solar system*. There is opportunity for classifying activities, from simply a list of the main objects—star, planets, moons, other satellites, comets, radiation, planetary rings, asteroids, etc.—to lists of various forms of matter, radiation, planetary surface conditions, kinds of moons, etc. The first two criteria can be met adequately, and the third—making some connection to our selves in a profound way—is also not very difficult to satisfy. The current search for water is tied with hopes of our traveling to and living on places otherwise impossible for us. The history of human discovery of the solar system from among the mass of lighted points in the night sky, the "outward urge" from our home planet to begin the adventure of becoming space travelers, the poetry and stories of space and of those objects most evident to our eyes—all are rich in material to evoke emotional engagement. The night sky's enchantment of human aesthetic senses can lead students to include Gustav Holst's *The Planets* in their portfolios—perhaps becoming the sound track for a presentation on *the solar system*. I have no doubt other cultures will have at least as rich resources with which to build a portfolio that, in time, can extend to include Western material, as Western students will extend into knowledge from other cultures.

Animals

This seemed initially like an easy topic, but it soon became obvious that it was too general; there was simply too much material, even though *animals* might satisfy the criteria developed so far. The "level" of a topic is clearly going to be important. While it might be tempting to say anything that is animal, vegetable, or mineral would make a suitable topic, other considerations interfere with that neatness. Not all animals will meet the criteria sketched so far. But the "level" comes into play in considering whether we should give one child the topic of *animals* or restrict it to, say, *tigers*. To indicate something of the "levels" problem we might then wonder whether *tigers* might be insufficiently varied and perhaps we might be better off with *cats*. *Cats* is, indeed, the better topic, allowing the student to explore the whole family of cats. Similarly, *horses* is clearly a good topic, because of the importance of the horse in human history and culture. A species that nearly died out six thousand ago is now to be found nearly everywhere because of its value to human beings—initially as an immensely powerful weapon and then as useful to all kinds of human enterprises. The horse appears in endless stories and poems, and Swift's *Gulliver's Travels* gives us a perspective on horses that delivers a disturbing perspective on ourselves. *Horses* is a good topic, but not all animals will be equally so. *Armadillos* isn't as rich a topic because of its marginality to general human history and culture, though I suppose the armadillo is more important to some cultures than is the horse, and if one's topic is *armor* one might include a close look at armadillos. Clearly some cultural sensitivity is required in concluding which animals, vegetables, and minerals will be suitable for children in different locations. So we are clearly going to have to select our animals, vegetables, and minerals one by one, being attentive to their associations with human history and culture—being aware that some animals that have played a small part in some cultures have enormously rich resonance within another. But this leads us to another criterion to add to our list: *topics must not be too general or too constrained (e.g.,* animal *is too general,* tiger *maybe OK, but* cats *is optimal.)*

Footwear

I confess that I had originally written "medieval footwear" and changed it early on as I realized that there probably wasn't enough information to keep students going for a dozen years! But with footwear in general there are a lot of styles to classify, they change over the ages, the anatomy of the foot becomes a part of the topic, and issues about the nature of style and changing fashions are raised. That is, the first criterion is satisfied, even if less obviously than in the case of some topics looked at above.

But a colleague, when I mentioned this among the topics, laughed and suggested a further criterion I had innocently not thought of. Any topic that is connected with fetishistic practices should probably be excluded. I guess that is a concern that one should be concerned about, even though it will be irrelevant for the most part. Even after giving this some thought, I can't say I am clear on what to do about it. I suppose, if one has the endless richness of the complexity of the world to give us topics, we don't need to include those that might be potentially problematic for some.

This problem also slides over to other topics that are likely to focus students' attention for too long on more discouraging features of human experience. In making the quick list that I'll examine below, I included *tools* and then immediately added *weapons*. But spending twelve years focusing attention on the variety of ways people have devised to maim and kill each other didn't seem likely to be entirely edifying. So out goes *weapons,* and I'm not sure what to suggest about *footwear,* medieval or otherwise, but in comes a further criterion to add to our growing list: *topics should not focus on the more depressing features of human existence.* Of course nearly all topics over twelve years of inquiry will lead to some information that is depressing in one way or another, but we needn't make that a central focus.

Teeth

I suppose one strike against *teeth* as a topic is that it might leave the students who study it for twelve years with little choice but to become dentists. But there does seem a lot to learn about teeth. Various animals and fish and even plants have teeth in many shapes and sizes. But is the variety great enough to keep a student engaged for twelve years? Maybe it fails to satisfy the criterion about not being too technical? The astonishing array of toothbrushes available for the care of teeth today certainly stimulates admiration for human ingenuity but somehow doesn't stir one to poetic effusions. I'm not sure the lore about teeth, or their place in literature and art, somehow provides the rich nimbus that would adequately satisfy our third criterion either.

But if not *teeth*, then perhaps some other body parts might earn a place on the list of suitable topics? *Ears, eyes*, the *heart*, the *gall bladder?* (Named for its inventor, Dr. Samuel Gall, according to Tom Lehrer's alarming account.) Of those, the *eye* and *heart* seem the more likely topics, but again they seem to fall by the criterion that requires richness of variety that is not too technical. Maybe the *eye* survives the criteria best.

Musical Instruments

This seems a simple winner. There is a huge variety of artifacts that people have pulled into the service of making music. Additionally, we can consider our bodies among the instruments we use to make music. We whistle, tap our fingers and feet, and we sing. All those activities will come into the study of the students who get *musical instruments* as their topic. I see no problem with this topic satisfying all the criteria easily.

One potentially troubling issue that this topic raises is a further criterion, that is: *every topic will offer students an equivalently rich experience.* They may all learn something in depth, but it may seem that learning about *musical instruments* in depth might be more fulfilling than learning about *dust* in depth. It is not enough to say that the purpose for which the LiD project is to be implemented in schools is satisfied by any topic that allows students to learn in depth. While that might be the case, and while such a scheme might provide an experience of learning that is a significantly different from what is generally available to students in schools today, it would seem a flaw in the proposal if it was clear that certain topics were in some sense much better than others.

Satisfying the third criterion—about the need to ensure that each topic will have dimensions of emotional engagement— should provide students with cultural, emotional, and imaginative meaningfulness whatever particular topic they get. But I think that this initial sense that *musical instruments* would be a prize topic to get and *dust* would be relatively dreary actually underestimates precisely what this scheme is supposed to teach; that is, that everything, studied in sufficient depth, is interesting; everything in which we can lose ourselves in learning can enrich our understanding and our imaginations. The assumption that some topics are privileged in this regard is, I think, largely a product of the superficial gaze at knowledge that is a curse of the current curriculum, and which this scheme is designed to overcome.

Even so, and while it has been an implicit criterion so far, it is perhaps worth making explicit the further criterion that each topic available for this scheme should enable each student to have an equivalently rich learning experience. That doesn't mean that each is on the surface equally attractive, but rather that each must satisfy all the criteria for suitable topics.

Ancient Persian Pottery

I added this topic somewhat whimsically, thinking of something fairly random and obscure that a student might nevertheless learn about in great detail over his or her years in school. Certainly we know a fair amount about such pottery, from fine bull heads to a huge variety of drinking and storage vessels. Those that are still in existence also include varied distinctive painted decorations, and many are witty, such as drinking vessels that are like the lower parts of a human body, resting on a couple of sturdy feet. On some of the earliest pieces one can still see the fingerprints of their makers, now as much as six thousand years old. That is, there is certainly quite a wide array of knowledge available about this topic, and distinctive forms of pottery were developed during the many ancient dynasties. However, knowledge about the topic is hardly as varied as what we know about apples or railroads.

There does appear to be a sufficient array of knowledge to satisfy the first criterion. My hesitation turns on the kind of knowledge it is, and how richly varied it is. I feel that this topic suffers a little in comparison to some of the more easily acceptable topics in much the way that the *rings of Saturn* failed. It's not so much that the knowledge available is largely technical, as seemed to be the case for the rings of Saturn, so much as some of the early classifying activities require a precision and sophistication that is unlikely to appeal to young children. Again, we will look at some of the ways we can deal with this problem in the next chapter, but the distinctions in kinds of pottery are not especially dramatic, and are made by specialists for specialists, with not a lot of play for the imagination of those who have not become intricately familiar with the topic. Though some of the artifacts we have are gorgeous, learning, for example, to distinguish different glazes that might enable us to make basic distinctions in our classifications doesn't offer hospitable grappling holds for children.

The second criterion is satisfied by the kinds of specialist detail one can accumulate. But, again, there is something a little constrained—compared to natural world topics—about the variety of areas one can plunge down into great detail. Also those areas of detail tend to require technical knowledge of a refined kind. There is something similarly constrained about the way the topic can satisfy the third criterion. Certainly the great beauty of many examples of the pottery feeds the soul, as it were, but it is not easy to see that there are other than aesthetic ties to our imaginations. Though, on the other hand, these ancient pottery pieces can feed our sense of wonder at human ingenuity.

I am being a bit tortured here because a topic such as this provides a helpful challenge to both the idea that *anything* can be successfully studied in the kind of the depth this scheme requires and that something that does indeed have an abundance of knowledge available might still be unsuitable because it requires too much technical knowledge to really get into it, and it seems to be too confining in the variety of access it can provide. Maybe, as with the *rings of Saturn*, if we decide that it is the specificity that is the main problem, we could more generally create a topic of *pottery,* and leave that much wider and varied array of artifacts for the students' exploration. And I am avoiding making the point that I suspect is in many readers' minds: how on earth does a child living in deprived economic, social, and intellectual conditions in a big city have any access at all to such a topic? If one accepts the mantra of "relevance to the student's experience," a topic such as this is off the radar. But, as will be evident from the previous chapter, part of the purpose of the LiD project is to show that access to knowledge is more varied than is dreamed of in the currently common assumptions about children's intelligence and the development of their imaginations and understanding.

: : :

By considering these unsuitable topics we have derived a few extra criteria we can use in selecting suitable topics for this project. But the discussion so far has given us only a dozen topics we might be able to use. What I have done for the next section is write down a set of further topics that seem to me likely suitable, and then to use them as starting points for identifying dozens of similar kinds of topics. They all seem to fit fairly well the criteria established so far. So I will see how easy it might be to generate similar kinds of topics, so that we can identify a hundred or so—the number of topics that I think would allow the project to get off the ground. It may be that just considering the varied topics below might allow us to identify thousands of potential topics. Let's see. The set below has been generated in about ten minutes, on a sunny November morning, grasping for seemingly possible topics out of the air.

Sacred Buildings

The first criterion is easily satisfied here as we have everything from the pyramids to international airport multifaith "prayer rooms" to Japanese teahouses within our subject matter. And in between there is a huge array of temples, churches, synagogues, etc. There is also an abundance of areas in which details might be pursued endlessly. There are possibilities for classifying sacred buildings: exploring their historical developments, how the forms of buildings are tied to beliefs, what clothing is considered appropriate for those ministering in the building and for those visiting it or attending a ceremony, and so on. Students might also study in further detail particular resonant buildings, of which there are many around the world.

The only small hesitation I have with this topic concerns how some parents, fervently committed to a particular religion, might see a study that looks at all sacred buildings as more or less equivalents, or parts of some historical developmental process that does not privilege theirs, might find it offensive. I recall from my own Catholic childhood, when I took it for granted that priests' and bishops' vestments were somehow derived from some holy source, that the discovery that they, and significant features of churches' design, had been taken over from the style adopted by imperial administrators during the later years of the Roman Empire came as a bit of a scandal. I know that's a trivial thing and shouldn't have any influence on someone's faith, but I wonder how learning in depth about the huge variety of beliefs people have fervently held might impact on religiously committed families. Schools implementing this proposal—if it ever comes to that—will likely face such concerns. In such cases *birds* or *apples* may come to their rescue.

If we allow *sacred buildings* as a topic, then maybe we could have *sports buildings* or *entertainment buildings?* These two seem to offer thin gruel compared with *sacred buildings,* so we might want to keep to topics that have the richer content and sets of associations. One of the topics I had added to this set earlier was *habitations.* I thought a good topic might be the kinds of building people had made to live in. *Houses* seemed to omit many kinds of habitations, and certainly would have excluded the earlier kinds, such as lean-tos and caves. *Habitations* has the possibility of easily satisfying the third criterion, as does *sacred buildings,* and they don't offend against any of the other criteria suggested above.

Water

This looks like another easy addition to the set of good topics. The only problem with this one is that it might be too rich in possibilities. We are, after all, just sacks for carrying water around so we can survive on land, as distinct from in the sea, which is our earlier home. Water is nearly everywhere on this planet; without water we can't survive for long. It is used in our religions and in endlessly varied forms in our drinks; it is what we think about when building houses—how to get it in and keep it out; we travel on it; it pours across the land in rivers; and on and on. *Rivers* can make a good topic by itself. *The water cycle* looks too much like a regular unit of study taught in all schools. But studied in depth over twelve years, *the water cycle* would be different indeed from the few-weeks-long unit that is commonly studied by students today.

I suppose one could have a general topic of *water* and also a separate one of *rivers*. If the student studying water chooses to look in detail at rivers, the focus would be quite different from that of the student who is looking exclusively at *rivers*. The latter may spend significant time looking at transportation on rivers, waterfalls, river life, and so on, which would likely not be brought into focus for the student studying *water* as a general topic.

So we might include a number of water-related topics as well as *water* itself. We can include *rivers,* and, on the same principle, *oceans* and perhaps *lakes and ponds.*

Cooking

The importance of cooking in human prehistory for the development of greater leisure is considerable—to the point that some see our arts as off-shoots of using fire to make food more readily digestible. Certainly cooking has involved a great range of implements and methods, and an astonishing range of plants, animals, and minerals have been subject to cooking. Cooking has nearly always entailed an occasion of social significance, sometimes to the point of religious importance. There is much to learn about the nutritional aspects of cooking, but also about its aesthetics, the economics in terms of energy and money and effort involved. There is evidence of roasting food among our distant ancestors as long as 750,000 years ago, and boiling food in pots has been common among human groups for at least 10,000 years. Those stretches of time give some resonance to the topic. There is no shortage of lore about cooking and the meals that result. Literature, poetry, and film provide sufficient richness to satisfy criterion three. The only danger with this topic, especially to the person who is an avid chef, is its vastness. But that is true of many of our topics, and I don't think *cooking* fails against any of the criteria so far established.

If we accept *cooking* as a straightforward topic, are there other similar prospective topics? To cook is to transform food by the application of heat; do we transform other objects in some related way for other purposes? *Buildings* comes to mind. *Buildings* might be a suitable topic, having the requisite variety, historical richness, and associations with our hopes and dreams. Maybe *furniture* is appropriate on the same grounds. Perhaps one might look at *decoration*, both for buildings and bodies. *Decoration* is a potentially useful topic for this project, in that it focuses on the things humans do that are useless from a functional point of view. It does seem to have rich resonances, and the challenge of engaging the five- or six-year-old is no greater than for many of our topics.

Tools

This is a little like some of the other topics that are technologies tied deeply into human cultures. The variety of tools is very great; human history is in significant part a story of their development and effects. From levers to hammers of various kinds, human functioning has been immeasurably augmented by our invention and refinement of tools.

The Measurement of Time

At one level this seems to be a constrained technical topic like some that were rejected above, in that one would be looking at the variety of technical tools with which people have tried to measure time. But this is potentially different from those others because of the nature of time itself. That is, there is an enriching mystery constantly nudging the student's attention as increasing knowledge is accumulated. One needs, perhaps, to be able to learn some knowledge about what is mysterious, rather than be unable to grasp what it is. And while the contrasts between Newtonian and Kantian views of time may engage philosophers, and will be engaging to our students in the later years of their study of this topic, they nevertheless suggest deep and enthralling mysteries that can capture the imagination quite early in one's contemplation of the topic.

As I wonder about this potential topic, I am increasingly inclined to want to include it when I think of the variety of ways people have tried to measure time in different cultures for different purposes. The mythologies of the world, and various religious traditions, have tried to account for time. So there is certainly no shortage of cultural material to work on, satisfying criterion three. There is also something odd about the way very ancient systems of counting time remain with us. (Why do we have sixty minutes in an hour, and twelve hours in a day, twelve in the night, and twelve months in a year? You don't know? Students who get this topic will. And why do we have so many words for two—brace, pair, twin, couple, deuce, double, binary, dual, dyad, etc.? Your homework for tonight.)

Are there other related topics this might encourage us to include? *Space* immediately suggests itself, or *the measurement of space.* This has a similar richness and is easily able to satisfy all of our criteria so far, as does *counting systems.* The huge variety of the world's counting systems exposes much about different human societies, and the methods of counting, in mathematics and music and everything else, expose fundamental features of our being and cultures.

Trees

Trees is another of those obviously satisfactory topics. It easily satisfies all of our criteria so far. The interest here is in what similar kinds of topics can be added. Immediately such topics as *grass* come to mind, and *flowering plants* (which will overlap somewhat with *trees*, as in "rhododendron," from the Greek for flowering tree). It wouldn't be hard to extend such a list through features of the natural world. And so we can include *whales, worms,* and *birds,* and many other animals. Or should we focus instead on classes of animals and insects? Perhaps *beetles,* rather than kinds of beetle, or *insects* rather than specific insects. (When J. B. S. Haldane was asked what he could infer about God from his creation, he said "He has an inordinate fondness for beetles"—one fifth of all known species are beetles.) That is, we need to hit the right level, as was established earlier, so that there is sufficient specificity but also sufficient variety. We also need to be attentive to the third criterion, which would be satisfied with, say, *ants* (because of the close relationship between ants and human communities for millennia) but not with *aphids.* But we can see how easy it would be to locate a large number of topics from the natural world: *wood* (as distinct from trees), *weather, volcanoes,* and *oceans.* Some colleagues suggested topics such as *wheat, rice, air, sun,* and *wind.*

I suppose one could, employing the same principle that allows both *water* in general and *rivers* in greater particularity, include *insects* and also some specific insects that can by themselves satisfy all the criteria, such as *ants and termites, beetles, bees and wasps, butterflies and moths,* etc.

Maps

Maps is another fairly straightforward winner, and it suggests a set of similar human-made topics: *flags and heraldry, games, writing systems and what people have written on, clothing and special clothing* (which would work in distinction from the more general topic of *clothing*—involving a focus on clothing that was specifically designed to mark off special offices, jobs, or roles), and *money*.

People and Places

This is a set of potential topics that raise a number of issues not dealt with so far. They would meet the criterion of having a sufficient amount of knowledge to keep someone learning for a long time. With regard to places, one could learn about current population and setting, about industries and trade, and about history. Take more or less randomly the town of *Salerno* in Italy. The history is extensive, with significant records from before ancient Roman times, when it became known as Salernum. But this richness of history would not be available to students who might be given the topic *Burnaby*—where my university is. The student who gets *Burnaby* instead of *Salerno* might instead study the history of the forest and its inhabitants who lived here for millennia, and this might also be adequately extensive to satisfy the criterion.

How does Salerno fare when it comes to the depth criterion? Certainly there are many opportunities for intensive studies of the lemon growing and trade and drinks that form a part of the region's income, of its geography and geology, and so on.

After thinking about this topic for a while, I think we should exclude both people and places as topics—even though I remain attracted by the idea of a student from south China driving down to Salerno from Naples for the first time when twenty years old, having studied the place for a dozen years. On the one hand people and places offer easy accommodation with all the criteria, yet on the other they can offer too intense attachments. They are, as a kind reader of the manuscript suggested, confusing in a different but related way to the reason they are excluded from Scrabble. Also one might be given or choose some heroic person to study, but the student over twelve years might go through the phenomenon very common to biographers. Often they set about writing the life story of someone they admire, but as the years of research go by, they increasingly come to loath the person the more they find out about him. Anyway, it is a possibly problematic area for topics.

Mind you, a more abstract use of places can become suitable topics, allowing us to include geographical features, such as *mountains, jungles, tundra, grasslands, fjords*, etc.

When I have solicited suggestions for further topics, I have received from a few people human qualities such as *loyalty, courage, love*, etc. I am not sure what to say about these. They do seem to satisfy the criteria established so far, but I feel uneasy about them. Maybe it is the abstractness. I don't know what the knowledge to be accumulated would be. One can imagine the study of courageous people and courageous acts, but it would seem to me more likely that gathering such accounts endlessly would indeed become enervating and boring—maybe it is the lack of variety that makes them unlikely to get past criterion two, and, to escape from endless anecdotage, one might be driven in the direction of philosophical or definitional inquiries into the nature of courage, or whatever. They might also fail to satisfy the criterion of uneasy generality. Maybe the failure of imagination here is mine; I can easily imagine a gathering of *birds* or *apples*, or even *dust*, students, but I'm not sure what the *courage* group might discuss or share, apart from yet more stories of courageous people or animals.

Criteria

When I have invited colleagues and teachers to suggest topics, it becomes immediately clear that there is no real problem about being able to indentify as many as we would need for almost any conditions. But the purpose of looking at so many potential topics here has been to articulate the criteria that should help us decide if a topic is going to be able to do the job this project requires.

In addition to the three principal criteria stated at the beginning of the chapter, this discussion has brought out a number of other important criteria to bring to bear on potential topics:

- sufficient width;
- sufficient depth;
- sufficient connections with the self—cultural, imaginative, and emotional ties;
- not too constrainedly technical;
- sufficient local resource materials available for adequate access;
- not too general or too unconstrained (e.g., *animals* is too general, *tigers* is maybe OK, but *cats* is optimal);
- not focused on the more depressing features of human existence nor on common phobias;
- each topic must provide an equivalently rich experience for all students;
- each topic must be acceptable to the student's parents or caregivers (i.e., matters of cultural sensitivity and ethics also need to be considered in the allotment or choice of topics).

Conclusion

Table 4.1, on pp. 124–25, presents some topics suitable for this project.

I suppose the one issue that remains a concern for me is the sense that natural world topics seem most readily to satisfy all the criteria, that *skin* is somehow better than *spacecraft,* that *goats* is better than the *printing press,* that *fish* is better than *robots,* that *bees* is better than *roads*—just to pick a few contiguous items from table 4.1. Maybe experience will help to clarify this, though I suspect that it will take a few years of students' building portfolios, and maybe more than a few, before any clear resolution one way or the other might appear.

This chapter is simply my attempt to work out what might serve as good topics to carry this program forward. Experience will also help to show up the shortcomings of my initial examples. These, after all, reflect my perspective and biases, personal and cultural, and these will be obvious to many readers who may be able to come up with a richer array of topics than I have. There is an obvious Western bias evident in the list and also, some have suggested, a gender bias. It will be easy to elaborate the list in ways that correct these faults in table 4.1, and we will use our Web site for this purpose, inviting anyone who wishes to send suggestions for additional topics. And the experience of trials will make clearer what kinds of topics work best. I do think the nine criteria are good guides to what will serve as topics, but some refinement even here will no doubt result from experience with implementations of the program.

Table 4.1. Some topics suitable for this project

Apples	Spiders	Dust	The wheel	Mollusks	Trains & railways	Rivers
The circus	Sacred buildings	Habitations	Water	Dogs	The Moon	Camels
Butterflies & moths	Teeth	Mushrooms	Tools	Measurement of time	Measurement of space	Tea
Ships	Grass	Trees	Flowering plants	Whales	Cats	Horses
Beetles	Insects	Ants	Maps	Wood	Icebergs & glaciers	Writing systems
Flags & heraldry	Volcanoes	Rice	Money	Navigation	Lakes & ponds	Spices
Birds	Special clothing	Edible roots	Air	Games	Jungles	Leaves
The solar system	Cooking	Silk	Worms	Apes & monkeys	Weather	Mountains
Olympic games	Theater	Islands	Exploration	Mills	Castles	The book
Bridges	Seeds	Sheep	Cattle	Counting systems	Rubber	Light

Agriculture	Jewels	Roads	Bees	Ancient ruins	Eggs	Weaving
Coral	Clouds	The submarine world	Electricity	Deserts	Photography	Rodents
Counting systems	Ponds & lakes	Robots	Fish	Wheat	Hands, feet, hooves, & paws	Storms
Stone	Dance	Spaces under the earth	Pirates	Inventors	Glass	Reptiles
Paper	Dyes	Wool	Wells	Tunnels	Cotton	Water transport
Mushrooms	Steel	Skin	Spacecraft	Submarines	Paints & their uses	Coffee
Frogs & toads	Pests	Color	Oil	The Arctic & Antarctic	Mail systems	Iron
Ice ages	Farm animals	The printing press	Goats	Gold	Tundra	Milk
Energy	Dams	Clocks	Bones	Coal	Food preservation	Savannah
Chemicals	Bears	Musical instruments	Aircraft	Carpets	Cereals	Irrigation

Some Operating Principles and Examples

5

A vulnerable part of this proposal is the initial steps. How do we manage to get the five-year-old, or the seven-year-old, sufficiently interested in dust or apples to get the project off the ground? What will they do for the first year or so?—especially if they can't yet read. Mind you, there are other vulnerable points, such as the major transitions that commonly take place in students' interests at around age eight—some time after fantasy worlds have evaporated, the Tooth Fairy and Santa Claus are long discarded with the dolls of childhood, and reality-based hobbies and collections begin. The other significant transition is at about age fifteen, when the hobbies and collections tend to be left behind in their turn and are replaced by a greater sense of independence and intense social life.

Building a portfolio over twelve years is going to involve a fair amount of hard work. What I want to do in this chapter is show how we can draw on sources of interest and energy in students to engage them with this work and enable them to see it as worthwhile.

I'll suggest some teaching principles we can use, derived in part from another project I have been engaged in. This one has involved a Vygotskian-oriented exploration of some of the socioculturally derived cognitive/psychological tools that students have available to make their learning most effective at particular phases of their educational development. Well, that's one way of putting it. Another would be to say that it has focused attention on what students find spontaneously engaging at different ages and then try to infer from their engagement more general principles that can be applied when teaching. Perhaps it will become clearer as I give some examples. In giving illustrations of the examples I'll continue to imagine a portfolio based on *apples*.

My purpose here is not to give descriptions of the kind of teaching approaches that can be found in many good books and Web sites. Rather I want to focus on approaches that may seem a little unusual at first but are well suited to this project and will be particularly helpful in engaging students' interest in their LiD topics.

Learning Tools for the First Years

The teacher who is supervising portfolios can draw on some of the following learning tools to engage students as they launch into their topic. These tools include the story form; binary opposites and mediations; forming images from words; metaphor use; puzzles and mystery; rhyme, rhythm, and pattern; and humor.

Take *the story form*. I don't mean fictional stories, though they are hardly to be excluded. Rather I mean "story" in the sense that we use the term about the evening news. What's the story on the bridge collapse, or what's the story on the election, on the movie star's latest behavioral extravagance, on the local team's struggle to win the cup, and so on? That is, we are not asking for fictional accounts of these topics. We want the facts, but we want them in a special form, in which the emotional importance of the facts is vividly brought out, and the facts are organized so that they have the greatest interest and impact. We can invite our young students to begin their topic, and can introduce them to it, by asking what's the story on dust, or leaves, or trains, or whatever. That is, we will be looking first for what is emotionally engaging about it, what can vividly capture their imaginations in their topic.

Portfolio supervisors need to develop a skill all good teachers are expert in: looking at topics in such a way as to engage students' imaginations in their content. They share this skill with the good reporter. "What's the story here?" If our topic is *apples,* the story has to do with the development from a restricted source of the remarkable variety currently available of this wonderfully healthy and delicious food, and has to do with how apples affect and have affected human lives. If that's central to our story, how do we get the young child into it? Well, let's see how we can draw on the help of some of the other learning tools.

We can use *binary opposites* to give the students a first and clear hold on the topic. Bruno Bettelheim noted the "manner in which [children] can bring some order into [their] world by dividing everything into opposites" (1976, p. 74). Once we have such oppositions in place, then we can mediate between them and gradually build a more adequate conception, but first we need to establish our binary grappling hooks. Imagine a world in which those wild apple trees in Kazakhstan were blighted seven thousand years ago and simply died out. Had that happened, we would now not have any apples; we would not be able to imagine the apple. So one binary opposite can be simply the *presence/absence* of apples, and we can encourage the child to consider how lucky we have been. We could choose less dramatic binary opposites to build our story on, of course. We might choose *sweet/sour,* or *rare/common,* or *human ingenuity in cultivation/chance development,* as oppositions onto which we can hang the astonishing story of apples.

We can also think about what *images* can get the child engaged in *apples,* or *dust* or *trains,* or whatever. By images I don't mean simply pictures, but rather emotionally charged senses that can be formed in their minds with words. We can have an image of a smell, for example. So I mean something more like an emotionally charged and perhaps diffuse association formed in the mind. The forming of one's unique images in the mind is one of the great early stimulants of the imagination.

So what emotionally charged images come to mind when we
think of the wonder of the mighty apple? Because apples are so
common today, with supermarkets carrying typically small mountains of as many as ten varieties, it is easy for students to take
them for granted. Also, of course, the abundant availability of
sugars, and the chemical industry's contribution to appealing to
the taste buds of children, reduces for children today the sense of
the deliciousness that apples held in the experience of children
in centuries past. So our first images should try to disrupt that
taken-for-granted image of apples as routine, plentiful, and not
especially tasty. We could tell students that in olden times visions
of paradise very commonly involved a garden in which fruit trees
were common (Hebrew, Chinese, Celtic, Germanic, Japanese,
Greek, African, etc.). Fruit was delicious and greatly prized, and
paradise was easy access to fruit. And of all the fruits in the world,
the apple has been the most highly prized. It is the most abun-
dantly produced fruit, and fruits are the most enjoyed nutritious
food, so the apple has been one of the world's most celebrated
foods. Later the students can learn that the word "fruit" is derived
from the Latin *fruor*, which means "I delight in."

An image suggested above is between the apple and paradise.
The very word "paradise" comes, via Greek, from the Persian
name for the walled gardens wealthy Persians built for themselves
long ago. Xenophon describes his amazement that throughout
the great Persian Empire the richest people had attached to their
homes large walled gardens in which they would grow flowers and
cedar, cypress, palm, and apple trees. The gardens were set usually in hot and arid landscapes and engineers directed water into
them, providing cool shade and greenery among predominantly
brown and tan surrounds. These gardens were called *pairidaeza*,
and represented security, calm, and beauty to their owners, and to
all who saw them—the walled garden being as close as one could
get to paradise on earth. The teacher can tell students about these
gardens in such a way as to call up in their minds this association
between the apple and the peaceful places in which they were
early cultivated. Pictures of such gardens can help build students'

images of such places and what they meant to their owners, as can stories that bring out the contrast between the harsh and arid world outside and the safety and green shade within—particularly appropriate stories chosen from *One Thousand and One Nights*.

Gradually the teacher can help build up other images, from the astonishing story of their elaboration from those early edible forms of apple in Kazakhstan thousands of years ago to the plump, rich, and juicy varieties available today. The image in the mind is of ingenious cultivation gradually plumping out with delicious fiber into multiple forms, colors, and flavors across the centuries. We might call up the image of some of the famous apple cultivators—perhaps the Etruscan Api—to make clear that this proliferation of varieties is an achievement of individual people, not some inhuman process of development. Or the image can be of the apple's interactions with our bodies: What happens when we eat one? If we are what we eat, what does the apple do for us? What amazing fact about apples suggests an image we can make important to the story we are to tell? The adventures of the wonderful apple can include William Tell and Johnny Appleseed and all those fairy tales that bring out the magic of the golden apples of the sun in memorable images.

Another of the great learning tools that comes along with an oral language is the ability to interpret and generate *metaphors*. This is a capacity of great importance to the elaboration of language. It's a somewhat magical and mysterious ability to see one thing in terms of another. Indeed, sometimes it seems as though we can see almost anything in terms of almost anything else: the tree of life, my heart is a stone, music is the food of love, the foot of the hill. You are probably familiar with those exercises that give two random lists of words and invite you to combine any two and explore the new meaning created.

The ability to recognize and generate metaphors seems to be very potent in young children (Gardner and Winner 1979), tied perhaps to the periods of most rapid language development. We get a hint of this power when we see a four-year-old playing with an empty box as a house, a car, a shoe, an airplane—all within a ten-minute period. So we will want to engage this metaphoric ability with the student's topic early on, so they can see it in numerous ways. An apple is literally a fruit, but metaphorically it can be a boat floating on a river to the sea, or a wholesome sign of friendship, or a computer logo, or a symbol of the theory of gravity, or an expression of appreciation to a good teacher, or anything we care to make it. We can help the students to keep a record of metaphoric uses of their topics and explore what these metaphors add to their understanding of it. The story of apples is truly one of progress—that powerful modern metaphor of development in a direction favorable to us.

The *sense of mystery* is another "tool" that comes along with language use. Language allows us to describe the world in symbols, and also to lie, to create fictions, and to articulate to others what we know. Mystery is an important tool in developing an engagement with knowledge that is beyond the students' everyday environment. It creates a sense of how much that is fascinating remains to be discovered. All the topics we might select have mysteries attached to them, and part of the teacher's job in making any topic engaging to students is to give them an image of richer and deeper understanding to draw their minds into the adventure of learning. Too often we represent the world to students as known, and we represent their task as to accumulate the knowledge that we already have. This is, of course, a part of education, but when we forget that our small circle of secure knowledge is bounded by a vast ocean of mystery, we make the educational task rather dull. When we make clear that we are engaged in a journey of discovery, surrounded by mystery, we better represent what the educational task is really like, and open up possibilities and wonder.

If our topic is apples, we can suggest a sense of mystery by picking up from the binary opposites—presence/absence—on which we can hang our story of apples. We might encourage the student to wonder about other fruits that might have existed in the distant past, but which did not survive. We have apples by chance, and others have certainly been lost by chance. What wonderful experiences, of taste and health, have we been deprived of? It needn't take much to stimulate the sense of mystery. That suggestion alone can be sufficient, if planted at the right time—to use a resonant metaphor. A small blight long ago might easily have deprived us of apples—what fruits, flowers, and trees were less lucky?

In addition we can wonder how many varieties of apple is it possible to develop, and what might future varieties include? What colors—those silver and gold apples? Can we expect bigger and bigger apples? How do the sun and earth astonishingly conspire to pack the colorful skin with healthy fiber? How magical is the neat skin, the rich pulp, and the seeded core? What mysterious changes it passes through on the branch, from bee-fumbled flowers to promising buds and then plumping out during the summer months to mellow fruitfulness till it ripely falls to the ground or is picked by grateful hands? How perfectly beautiful the many hued varieties are, especially when gathered in baskets or barrels or on the table in bowls—rich metaphors of nature's beneficence. Why are apples used in many religious traditions as a mystical or forbidden fruit?—so many ancient stories combine the seductiveness of apples, to which people succumb, with some punishment for giving in to such sweet temptation. We can find ways in which even the young child can be introduced to this mysterious dimension of apples by telling some of these stories, and pointing out that this unexpected connection recurs in different stories.

Rhyme, rhythm, and pattern are potent tools for giving meaningful, memorable, and attractive shape to any topic. Their roles in learning are numerous, and their power to engage the imagination in learning the rhythms and patterns of language—and the underlying emotions that they reflect—is enormous. They are important in learning all the forms of knowledge and experience that we code into symbols. So we will want to find the more vivid and dramatic rhymes, rhythms, and patterns connected with any particular topic. We can start with simple nursery rhymes. If *apples* is our topic, we can begin a file with such near-nonsense rhymes as:

Do you like apples, do you like pears?
Do you like tumbling down the stairs?

That one, mysteriously, kept our children in belly hugging laughter for years, as each went through the magical point of language development for which it worked so well.

Teachers can invite physical participation with such rhymes as:

Five red apples
Hanging on a tree [*five fingers held down*]
The juiciest apples you ever did see!
The wind came past
And gave an angry frown [*shakes head and looks angry*]
And one little apple came tumbling down.
Four red apples . . .

And here's an item for those mastering the alphabet:

A Was an Apple Pie
A was an apple pie,
B bit it,
C cut it,
D dealt it,
E eat it,
F fought for it,
G got it,
H had it,
I inspected it,
J jumped for it,
K kept it,
L longed for it,
M mourned for it,
N nodded at it,
O opened it,
P peeped in it,

Q quartered it,

R ran for it,

S stole it,

T took it,

U upset it,

V viewed it,

W wanted it,

X, Y, Z, and ampersand

All wished for a piece in hand.

Taken gratefully from
http://www.mamalisa.com/blog/?p=327.

Jokes and humor can expose some of the basic ways in which language works and, at the same time, allow students to play with elements of their topic, so discovering some of learning's rewards. This learning tool can also assist the struggle against arteriosclerosis of the imagination as students continue through their schooling—helping to fight against rigid conventional uses of rules and showing students rich dimensions of knowledge and encouraging flexibility of mind. It's always easy to begin with such simple items as:

Q: When is an apple not an apple?

A: When it's a pair [pear].

To "get" the joke one has to be able to see that the same sound often does double duty, and so one begins increasingly to see language as an object and not just as an unreflective behavior. That ability to see language as an object we can reflect on is central to developing what scholars call "meta-linguistic awareness," and that ability in turn is implicated in learning to use language with flexibility and sophistication. So jokes are not just good fun, but they are also what Lévi-Strauss called *bons-à-penser*—good things for thinking; they have the potential to enlarge our understanding and language fluency.

There are, of course, endless more conventional kinds of apple jokes, such as:

The children were lined up in the cafeteria of a Catholic elementary school for lunch. At the head of the table was a large pile of apples. The nun made a note, and posted it on the apple tray: "Take only ONE. God is watching."

Moving further along the lunch line, at the other end of the table was a large pile of chocolate chip cookies. A child had written a note, "Take all you want. God is watching the apples."

Or an example perhaps not ideal for school, though the students will like it:

Physics Teacher: Isaac Newton was sitting under a tree when an apple fell on his head and he discovered gravity. Isn't that wonderful?

Student: Yes. If he had been sitting in class looking at books like us, he wouldn't have discovered anything.

: : :

This set of learning tools—the story form; binary opposites and mediations; forming images from words; metaphor use; puzzles and mystery; rhyme, rhythm, and pattern; and humor—can be used to engage the young students with their topics. They are hardly an exhaustive set, and I have no doubt that experienced teachers will be able to add a number of their own that will be at least as effective as some of these. It's just that these tools can help us to recognize that beginning to explore a randomly assigned topic needn't be haphazard, leaving students wallowing and easily bored. We can engage their interest in *apples* or *the circus* or *birds* or whatever by bringing out the story about the topic and thereby showing what is emotionally important about it; we can provide them with grappling tools in the form of binary opposites; we can capture their imaginations with vivid, affectively charged images; we can encourage flexibility and vividness of understanding by play with metaphors; we can find puzzles in their topic and surround it with an alluring sense of mystery; and we can enliven students' interest by drawing attention to rhymes, rhythms, patterns, and jokes.

I haven't dwelt much on that commonly used cognitive tool that develops with language use, and that's the puzzle or problem. This tool is perhaps too familiar to need much elaboration, but setting up problems or puzzles can stimulate students' explorations in many directions. The teacher can constantly raise questions that may encourage students to develop further pieces of knowledge, even if initially the knowledge is only very general and imprecise: How many different kinds of apple can you find? Where do their names come from? Do apples float—why or why not? What is your favorite apple? Where do the apples you buy come from? How many colors can apples be? How many songs and stories and nursery rhymes mention apples? Why are apples good for us to eat? And so on. One of the larger implementation programs currently underway began by giving each student their topic and three questions about it to get them going.

Table 5.1 presents a summary of learning tools for the early years.

Table 5.1. Some prominent learning tools students from K to grades 3/4 can use in building their portfolios

Story	One of the most powerful tools students have available for engaging with knowledge. Stories shape our emotional understanding of their content. Stories can shape real-world content as well as fictional material.
Binary opposites	Basic and powerful tools for organizing and categorizing knowledge. We see such opposites in conflict in nearly all stories, and they are crucial in providing an initial ordering to many complex forms of knowledge.
Images	Generating mental images can be immensely engaging in exploring knowledge. They can attract our emotions and imaginations to aspects of any topic. The use of mental images (as distinct from external pictures) should play a large role in stimulating students' interest in their topics.

Metaphors	Enable us to see one thing in terms of another. This peculiar ability lies at the heart of human intellectual inventiveness, creativity, and imagination. It is important to help students keep this ability vividly alive by exercising it in building their portfolios.
Mystery	An important tool in developing engagement with knowledge that is beyond the student's everyday environment. It creates an attractive sense of how much that is fascinating remains to be discovered. All topics have mysteries attached to them, and part of the teacher's job in making exploration of their topics more engaging to students is to give them an image of the richer and deeper understanding that is there to draw their minds into the adventure of learning.
Rhyme, rhythm, and pattern	These are potent tools for giving meaningful, memorable, and attractive shape to any content. Their roles in learning are numerous, and their power to engage the imagination in learning the rhythms and patterns of language is enormous.
Jokes and humor	Can expose some of the basic ways in which language works and, at the same time, allow students to play with elements of knowledge, so discovering some of learning's rewards. They can also assist the struggle against arteriosclerosis of the imagination as students continue to build their portfolios.
Puzzles and problems	Pointing out puzzles or problems can stimulate students' explorations in many directions. The teacher can raise questions that encourage students to encounter some attractive difficulty, solving which will enable them to develop further knowledge.

Learning Tools for the Middle Years

Once students become fairly efficiently literate, reading and writing with ease and using many of the above tools in organizing and classifying knowledge, some new cognitive tools come into play. One way to think about the shift to literacy is to see it in terms of a shift from a dominance of the ear to the eye in gathering information (Havelock 1963, 1986; Innis 1951; Ong 1982). Literacy is commonly thought of as a more or less complex skill, whereas we might better think of it as a tool kit, invented a few thousand years ago, and accessible now to anyone who learns to use those tools appropriately. Literacy brings with it a whole range of additional learning tools that we commonly don't think of when we focus on simply the coding and decoding aspect of it. Here, I want to focus on the often-neglected tool kit that comes along with literacy.

Certain activities can facilitate this shift from ear to eye and also show students how literacy can give new powers with the accumulation of new learning tools. Usually we see these changes begin to come into prominence at about ages seven, eight, or nine. So the supervisors of students' portfolios at these ages might be alert to signs of students spontaneously using the kinds of tools I will describe below, and might then help students to begin to reorganize the information they have already accumulated in their portfolios in more efficient, eye-dominant forms. In particular, this might be the time to develop students' digital online portfolios—perhaps even to the point of scanning or taking digital photos of earlier drawings or pictures and having them available in the student's portfolio server space. (I'll discuss this in more detail later.) Attention should be given to helping students reorganize their portfolios, and to prepare categories and file systems that will be more effective in dealing with the increasing knowledge, and the new kinds of knowledge, which students will gain in this period.

During these years, the worlds of fantasy fade away and are replaced in some degree by the light of common day, or with what adults recognize simply as a more realistic view of things. Santa and the Tooth Fairy yield to fantasy creatures of a different kind, whom students don't believe are true in the same way, and they yield also to real-world heroes. This new sense of reality does seem to be influenced by particular forms of literacy. As Jerome Bruner puts it: "literacy comes into its full powers as a goad to the redefinition of reality" (1988, p. 205).

So we see in the kinds of stories that most readily engage students a new concern with reality. Anne of Green Gables and the
rabbits of *Watership Down* make quite different accommodations
with reality than did Cinderella or Peter Rabbit. Even such fantasies as Superman, Spiderman, the Hulk, and their equivalents
all come with elaborate explanations for the fantasy elements
of the stories, suggesting that they fit into some kind of reality;
fairy godmothers are simply asserted, but Superman needs an explanation, however impossible we might find the account of his
escape from exploding Krypton and so on. An oddity of much educational literature at the moment is the suggestion that one can
best engage students' interest by starting with what they already
know and is a part of their everyday environment. I have earlier
suggested why this is odd in the context of what seems to be most
interesting to typical students at these ages—those spies, pirates,
star warriors, superheroes, etc. (Yes, they "know" some aspects
of these—but if this is all the principle is supposed to tell us, it
doesn't tell much.)

The everyday world around students is not apparently what
they find most interesting, rather it is *the extremes of experience
and the limits of reality* that most powerfully engage students'
imaginations as literacy becomes fluent. That is, the reality that
we first engage imaginatively during these years tends to focus on
the extremes, on its most exotic and bizarre features, on the most
terrible and courageous events. We are familiar with this kind of
material from sensational newspapers, from TV shows, and from
publications like *The Guinness Book of Records*. Supervising teachers might sensibly be alert, then, to how to use this learning tool
of engagement with the extremes and limits of reality and experience in expanding students' portfolios in new directions and dimensions. (The attention to the extremes and limits of reality, to
the exotic, weird, and bizarre, is not disconnected with students'
everyday reality; rather it is how they establish the context of their
everyday reality and, in some deep sense, its meaning.)

If the topic is apples, students might be encouraged to begin
exploring the largest and smallest kinds of apples, the rarest, those

that have been cultivated for the most extreme climates, those that last longest after being picked and those that wither fastest, the sweetest and sourest, and so on. A student might open a file on "apple records" to contain such information. Where are the largest orchards, and to whom do they sell their apples? How are they transported? How many tons of apples were grown worldwide last year, and how does this compare with previous years? How many of those original orchards in central Asia continue to produce apples? Are they in danger? The exotic and extreme can be routes to massive amounts of engaging information.

During the years from around eight to around fourteen or fifteen, students feel increasing independence, but are typically hemmed in by rules and regulations that they commonly find irksome. They see much that they want and much that they want to be, and remain relatively powerless to gain either. A learning tool that becomes quite prominent during this period is *the ability to associate with heroic qualities*. We identify as heroes those people who are able to overcome the threats that hem us in, constraining us from gaining those things we dream of. We lack the money or power or skill to achieve what we would like, so we associate with those who most clearly have the heroic qualities that enable them to achieve precisely what we want. It is a tool that helps us overcome our insecurities; it enables us to overcome some of the threat of alienation involved in the new sense of reality. By associating with those things or people that have heroic qualities we can gain confidence that we too can face and deal with the real world, taking on those qualities with which we associate.

The story of William Tell gains a new resonance for students at this age. They want to know now about the real person behind the story. Johnny Appleseed is a mythic figure who reflects the heroic activity of real people who spread apple trees and cultivated new varieties; it is now time to introduce the true stories of the real people who carried apples across North America, bringing to the fore the real heroes in this epic tale. Who made the greatest contributions to the development of the apple from ancient times to the present? Are the most widely cultivated apples recently developed? What is happening to those older varieties of apple that are not suitable for modern forms of transportation and supermarket sales—are there heroic people working to preserve varieties? Who and where? The apple itself can be seen as heroic: a vulnerable plant like many that have disappeared over evolutionary time, which overcomes its vulnerability in one small and remote area of the world to spread and proliferate across the planet.

Grasping knowledge through human emotions is another tool that enables us to get beyond the surface of any knowledge to its source in human emotion. All knowledge is human knowledge, discovered or invented as a result of some human emotion. This tool allows us to see knowledge through the emotions that were involved with its past creation or current use, and so grasp its deeper human meaning. We often forget that during the ages from about eight to fifteen, students make sense of the world very largely in personal terms; not personal simply in the sense of their own local interests, but rather in the sense that it is through seeing knowledge in terms of universal human feelings that it gains much of its meaning.

This learning tool also encourages us to direct students' attention to the people involved in the story of apples, or whatever the topic is. Who were the cultivators? What were their motives? Who developed orchards and against what opposition or threats? Who discovered the health benefits of apples, and how did they feel about their discoveries? In all such cases we are asking, again, what's the story here, or what narrative can we discover that shows the emotional meaning of the knowledge being learned.

The *sense of wonder* is another key learning tool in our initial explorations of reality. It enables us to focus on any aspect of the world around us, or the world within us, and see its particular uniqueness. It serves as a spotlight, bringing something into bright focus while somewhat suppressing everything else. We can turn this sense of wonder onto anything, recognizing the wonderful in each feature of the world: "everything is wonderful." This tool can provide the gift that allows us to recognize something wonderful behind even the most routine and taken-for-granted things. The starting point of all science and all inquiries is "I wonder why . . ." It gives us the ability to imbue any aspect of reality with heightened importance.

The story of the apple is replete with wonders—historical, medicinal, technical, "orchardic," etc. Students can begin to explore the apple in greater detail, focusing on just what are its healthful properties, how it grows, its roles in history and art, its development around human settlements, its fruity competitors for our palette and their various pros and cons, and so on.

Around age seven or eight one of the more curious activities of nearly all children begins. They commonly start to collect something or start a hobby. What is going on? Well, one explanation is that they are seeking some security in this new world of reality in which they find themselves; that world might be infinitely extensive and by getting control of some small part of it, through their collection or hobby, they gain some security that it isn't, at least, infinite. These hobbies commonly continue till around age fourteen or fifteen.

The learning tool that is tied in with *collections and hobbies* can find energetic work to do in expanding students' portfolios during this period. If the topic is *apples*, then one might look for features of apples that open them up to the collecting instinct. This might be the time for the development of relational tables of all the variety of apples the student can discover, or elaborate "family trees." The online portfolio can have pictures of as many varieties as can be found. (I'm not sure what real artifacts connected with apples might be collected for the physical portfolio: perhaps photographs of all the apples and apple tree varieties the student has located? Pressed leaves from various trees? I was going to add as a kind of joke "pips," assuming they would all look much the same but maybe some of our apple experts might indeed be able to distinguish features of pips.)

The kind of intellectual energy one sees being spent on students' hobbies and collections can also be harnessed to expand and alter somewhat the work they do on their portfolios. Ideally, their portfolios will become a kind of hobby or collection during these years from around seven or eight to fourteen or fifteen.

Changing the context is a tool that enables the imagination to grasp a richer meaning of any topic. The classroom is often an emotionally sterile place; so routine that one topic after a while begins to look like another. By shifting the context in which knowledge is learned—often by use of simple devices—students' imaginations can be brought vividly to life, engaging the material much more richly.

As students begin to develop this intermediate tool kit, the portfolio supervisor can deliberately encourage them to take different perspectives on their topics from those that dominate the portfolio to this point. The aim is to see the topic in many contexts, through many perspectives. If they haven't done so already, they might be encouraged to start looking at the biology of apples, or their medicinal properties, or discover uses of apples in myth stories or other fictions, to explore the history of the apple, to study apples in art and perhaps to try to copy paintings and then do their own life studies, to attend to the ideal climatic conditions for different varieties, to monitor and note the decay of different varieties of apple, and so on.

:::

At around age seven or eight, many students' spontaneous interests change quite significantly, and the kinds of stories they enjoy also change. These changes are clues to some of the new learning tools we can use to refresh their interest in their topics and draw them to expand it into new dimensions. We need to recognize that improved literacy brings with it a somewhat distinctive conception of the reality the students find themselves in. Their interest in their topics can be enlarged by a focus on extremes and limits, on the strange and exotic, on "records" associated with it. Knowledge tends to become more engaging if seen in the context of human lives and the human emotions that students share, and especially if they can see new aspects of their topic through the heroic qualities of people involved with it. We will want to draw their attention to the wonderful features of their topics—to those things that are attractive because of their unusualness or because they transcend the everyday. We will also seek to show them that their topic has features that can engage the collecting instinct or can be like a hobby. These learning tools remain prominent in students' "tool kits" till around fourteen or fifteen.

Table 5.2 presents a summary of learning tools for the middle school years.

Table 5.2. Some prominent learning tools students in the middle years of schooling can use in building their portfolios

The sense of reality	The development of rational and logically structured forms of thinking is greatly eased by literacy, and these can be deployed to restructure students' portfolios.
The extremes of experience and the limits of reality	Students' imaginations grasp reality readily in terms of its limits and extremes; they focus on the extremes, on the most exotic and bizarre features of reality, on the most terrible and courageous events. These features can add a new dimension to students' portfolios.
Associating with heroes	Enables students to overcome some of the threat of alienation involved in the new sense of reality. By associating with those things or people that have heroic qualities, we can gain confidence that we too can face and deal with the real world, taking on those qualities with which we associate. It gives us a further tools to explore human dimensions of portfolio topics.
The sense of wonder	We can turn this sense of wonder onto anything, recognizing the wonderful in every feature of the world. This tool can provide the gift that allows us to recognize something wonderful behind even the most routine and taken-for-granted things. The starting point of all science and all inquiries into all topics can be "I wonder why . . ."
Grasping knowledge through human emotions	Enables us to see beyond the surface of any knowledge to its source in human emotion. All knowledge is human knowledge, discovered or invented as a result of some human emotion. This tools allows us to see knowledge through the emotions that were involved with its past creation or current use, and so grasp its deeper human meaning.

Narrative understanding	A narrative context for knowledge can establish its emotional importance while also conveying the knowledge—about any topic. It keeps alive the sense of the "story" the student is investigating.
Collections and hobbies	The drive to exhaustively discover something to give us security in a complex world. This tool can be harnessed to allow students to explore aspects of their topics in great detail.
Changing the context	By shifting the context in which knowledge is learned—by use of often simple devices—students' imaginations can be brought vividly to life, engaging the material in new dimensions.
Early tools of literacy: the list, etc. "The imaginative eye."	The shift to literacy reflects also a shift from a dominance of the ear to the eye in gathering information. Certain activities can facilitate this shift and also show students how literacy can give new powers. One of the most basic of these activities can be demonstrated through the making and manipulation of lists, and of flowcharts, diagrams, etc.

Learning Tools for the Final School Years

By around fifteen years of age students who have continued to elaborate the set of learning tools described above commonly experience another quite fundamental shift in their understanding, which can be described in terms of some new learning tools they prominently deploy. The most evident index of this further tool kit is the use of a new vocabulary in which theoretic abstractions become common. Earlier in their lives, for example, students would have known the meaning of a word like "nature." They would have thought of it in terms of animals and woodlands, the sea and birds, and so on. What begins to happen at the transition to this new kind of understanding is development of such general ideas as "nature" so that it is seen increasingly less in terms of particular features and more as a complex system; it is as though the connections between the features of the natural world become more prominent than the individual features themselves. Similarly a whole range of facts and ideas and knowledge take on a new sense and significance by being seen as elements of general *processes* rather than as simply more or less interesting elements.

I hope this isn't too abstract a way of putting it, and that it is clear how this new theoretic way of thinking is distinct from the forms of thinking that were shaped by the previous set of learning tools. The shift becomes clear in the way students begin to form theories of history and society, ideologies, metaphysical schemes, and so on. They begin to build a new theoretic world, which they populate with these abstractions. Or, at least, one may see this in students who have successfully managed the earlier stages of schooling, and perhaps less evidently in those who have managed less well. But students who will by this time have accumulated significant portfolios are more likely to be making this transition to a more theoretic kind of understanding than may be true of the average student today.

An example might help introduce what I mean. I remember driving our sons to soccer when one was about thirteen and the other sixteen. We were coming up to a federal election, and many of the lawns and windows we passed had sprouted posters in bright red, blue, yellow, and green encouraging us to vote for one or another candidate and party. In the election four years earlier, my children had been interested in how many signs were up for "our" candidate, in who had the most signs and the biggest signs, in which party was likely to win, and in how anyone could vote for the villains who opposed our good guys. Putting his soccer boots on in the car, on this later occasion, our older son asked whether we had to pay to have a sign on our lawn, and whether people with the really big signs had to pay more, or did the candidates pay us to put signs on our lawns. I told him that the candidates and their parties paid to have the signs made, or made them themselves, and people put them on their lawns freely to show their support. "But why would people vote for some party because of a sign on a lawn?" one of them reasonably asked, adding, "Wouldn't people vote based on their principles, rather than be swayed by lawn signs?" We discussed this for a while, and their questions spread to the ways in which lawn signs were a part of the process of democratic elections.

My point is to indicate an example of a shift in thinking and in the set of cognitive tools being brought into play. And my purpose here isn't to try to explain *why* this change occurs, typically in the mid-teens among students who have continued to develop the sets of learning tools discussed above, but rather to describe some of its features in a way that illustrates how teachers might engage the *theoretic* imagination in learning. (An attempt at explaining *why* this change occurs can be found in Egan 1997.)

The sense of abstract reality is a tool that develops as a part of the development of rational, logically structured forms of thinking. It has historically been the source of our understanding of the processes by which nature works, and our increasing control over these processes, but can come at the cost of our alienation from the natural world—so that we might see nature, for example, only as a set of "resources." The students' portfolio supervisors can use, and encourage in students the use of, the abstract language of the theoretical world. A dictionary of word origins can be invaluable for elaborating on the etymology of theoretic language, and thereby supporting the development of theoretic learning tools.

So the student might be encouraged to explore pomology, perhaps by going to the Web sites of universities where there are departments devoted to the study of fruits, and perhaps later by visiting such institutions. What are the current interests of scientists dealing with pomology? What are "replant diseases," and how are they being treated? What are the conflicting theories involved in treating them? And what is the best way to deal with codling moth infestations? What are the underlying theories that lead to different approaches? There are hundreds of similar topics and issues, and theoretical disputes that *apple* students will by now be ready and probably eager to join. They might alternatively become fascinated with the representation of apples in art and literature, discovering how apples serve as symbols of amorous, aesthetic, or religious meanings and the ways in which they appear and play roles in courtship, domestic life, and art.

The *sense of agency* is a cognitive tool that enables us to recognize ourselves as related to the world via complex causal chains and networks. So we can become more realistic in understanding how we may play roles in the real world, and understand ourselves as products of historical and social processes. This realization that our very sense of self is a product of the social and historical conditions that have shaped the world around us is often quite disturbing to students even while increasing a sense of intellectual potency. Portfolio supervisors can increasingly look for ways to encourage students to take part in activities that will help stimulate their sense of agency. The aim would be to help students to look "outward" from their portfolios and see how the knowledge they have been accumulating can be brought to bear in the real world.

The student can begin to engage in a range of social or even political activities connected with apples (or with whatever the student's topic is). Perhaps the student may have concluded that the reduction in the available apple varieties in supermarkets is potentially dangerous, should some disease devastate one or more of the commonest varieties. The student could be encouraged to write to owners of orchards, first seeking their views on the greatly reduced varieties currently grown, and see whether they think it is a problem, and to consider the orchardists' reasons carefully. If the student still thinks there are real dangers in the reliance on so few varieties, she can be encouraged to write letters to her political representative to express her concern. She can join groups who are taking action to preserve a greater variety of apples. She might conclude that the quantity of pesticides currently used in apple cultivation is in excess of what is needed and poses both an environmental threat and possibly may be leading to some damage to apple stocks and to many of the harmless life forms that would normally exist along with apples. After hearing the case of the orchardists, if she still concludes there is a potential danger, she could join political action groups that lobby for reductions and controls over pesticide use and other chemicals that lead to more profits for apple producers but at a risk the student reasons is excessive and indeed risks future profits. She might explore sources of public information about chemical and insecticide use in orchards, and engage in what she concludes are appropriate public actions to inform others and to lobby political representatives. Alternatively, of course, her public actions might be engaged in on the side of the orchardists and growers. What matters is the movement from knowledge to related public action. What also matters is that the action be recorded in one or another form or medium and be added to the student's portfolio.

British gardeners, in particular, keep a wide variety of apples in cultivation, but most of the apple varieties that existed in the United States a hundred years ago are now gone, in favor of the few commercially profitable varieties in which "shelf life" has been considered more important than taste. Taste is often sacrificed by picking apples too early, allowing them to ripen under artificial conditions on the way to market, rather than on the tree. The student can become active, by writing letters, seeking interviews and learning the problems the farmers experience, and perhaps making the case to the farmers for adding some varieties to their orchards, using data they have available in their portfolios.

The student might look for the opportunity to grow apple trees and to learn how to propagate them. Often allotments are available near cities for those who lack space around their homes. The student might make contact with pomology departments of universities, locally or online. She can request information about current research projects, and ask whether there might be a role for a knowledgeable volunteer. Perhaps she might, in her dream job, even be able to travel with a research group to Kazakhstan to study the health of the original apple trees, perhaps counting grubs on leaves, or doing some grunt work that can add importantly to knowledge. She might be able to do such work more locally, of course.

General theories and their anomalies is a tool that enables us to generate abstract ideas about nature, society, history, and human psychology, and then recognize their inadequacy, and rebuild them into more complex ideas. How does this work? I have described very briefly above that a distinctive feature of this new tool kit involves forming theories, and some of these are very general and often simplistic. So one finds students quite suddenly sometimes beginning to think about whether the world is getting better or worse within a huge historical time frame. If, for example, the student begins to shape a theory of history that is optimistic, seeing, almost in a Victorian sense, progress in action in all spheres of life, then there are some facts that will be anomalous to this view; some facts will clearly run counter to it. So the fact of Third World poverty, despite excessive affluence in some parts of the world, is an anomaly to the optimistic general theory. The student's theory need not be disproved by such a fact, though. The student can make the theory more sophisticated or nuanced, claiming that the general progress of the world is not regular, and so incorporate the anomalous fact. But it might then be pointed out that those deprived areas become a threat to the "developed world" because of their resentment and armed hostility, and also because poverty breeds diseases that are then transmitted around the globe and threaten massive destruction to all societies. The theory then needs to be made more sophisticated again to accommodate these further anomalies. And so the process of general schemes being threatened by anomalies and the anomalies forcing the general schemes to become more sophisticated to accommodate them, and so, dialectically, on, is one of the tools we can see at energetic work as students build their theoretic worlds.

The project supervisor at this stage needs to be alert for students beginning to develop the most general theories concerned with apples and their place in the human and natural worlds. One realm for rich theory development, to continue examples from above, is the battle between modern intensive orchard cultivation and the dangers, under market pressures, of reducing the varieties and taste of cultivated apples, and also the threats created by massive use of chemical insecticides and fertilizers. Perhaps the student might form a theory about organic methods of apple production. Anomalies to that theory will include the problems of producing enough apples to meet market demands and also adequately controlling apple pests. Learning more about these anomalies will compel the student to develop an increasingly sophisticated theory of organic production of apples. The aim in raising anomalies, which may become a significant task for the supervisor—but we can also rely on the students' own accumulating knowledge to throw up these anomalies as well—is not to overthrow the student's theories, but rather to make them more and more sophisticated. While the student might begin with idealistic views, the gradual accumulation of anomalies might lead her to conclude that current industrial apple production ensures good tasting fruit made accessible to everyone at a low cost.

The search for authority and truth is a further tool that takes on a particular shape and importance with the development of abstract theoretic thinking. Because meaning is seen to be derived from general ideas, it becomes vital to determine which ideas are true. An objective, certain, privileged view of reality is sought. Among the historical products of this cognitive tool at work have been dictionaries, encyclopedias, and textbooks—repositories of secured knowledge.

The sense that truth and meaning are to be located first in the general and abstract drives the theoretic thinker constantly, even if subconsciously sometimes, to look for the abstract source in which authority and truth can be located. If the abstract thinker loves singing, it will no longer be sufficient to simply prefer one singer to another. He will draw up criteria for goodness in singers, and compare singers in terms of these criteria. As theoretic thinking becomes more sophisticated, this becomes a tricky business. Maria Callas or Britney Spears may seem best according to some criteria, but Cecilia Bartoli or Ani DiFranco better according to others. Perhaps one should have different criteria and categories for contraltos and sopranos or for different genres of music? Or if the student begins to think theoretically about something as mundane as shopping, he might wonder whether shopping has replaced religion for some people, or whether the economic benefits derived from consumption of certain goods that do little for the lives of many consumers are offset by spiritual desiccation and environmental degradation, or not. They will reflect on how we could reliably compare such things. What are the benefits to our patterns of shopping compared to the way people in oral cultures gathered what they needed and wanted? How can one find the "true" answers to such questions?

Our student who is building a portfolio about apples may use this tool to drive inquiries into the truth about variety reduction, or the adequacy of the criteria for establishing what counts as a new variety of apple, or whether Newton was really stimulated in his thinking about gravity from watching an apple fall, or any of an indeterminate array of issues that may seem to have discoverable and certain conclusions. The student's portfolio supervisor might be alert to such questions in case the student may be hesitant in taking on this more theoretic approach to her or his topic.

Meta-narrative understanding is a tool that allows us to order particular facts or events into general ideas and form emotional associations with them. That is, we don't just organize facts into theories, but our tendency to shape even our theories into more general meta-narratives also shapes our emotional commitments to them. For example, think of the different meanings and emotional associations that emerge when we try to make sense of the destruction of the World Trade Center's twin towers on September 11, 2001, from mainstream American and Middle Eastern Islamic perspectives. In the West, this event fits commonly into a meta-narrative in which it can be made sense of only as an evil act of terrorists, in response to which a "war on terrorism" is justified. In a militant Islamic meta-narrative, the oppressive Western "devils" were being struck by heroic soldiers of God who sacrificed their lives rather than accept continual oppression and the suppression of their values and way of life. This example illustrates how a meta-narrative is not just a logical structuring device but is primarily responsible for orienting emotions to the topic. No one is disputing the central facts or events. It is their meaning that is shaped by the meta-narrative an individual is using.

The student's supervisor might be alert to the main meta-narratives commonly used in making sense of the topic. Even apples will be subject to some meta-narratives. The student might be encouraged to question whether the current abundance of apple varieties and the vast orchards in China, the United States, and Russia represent a perversion of an organic development of plants in general. Woodlands and varied grasslands have been obliterated to grow an overabundance of a fruit that has helped degrade the biodiversity of the planet. Alternatively the student can shape the knowledge so far gathered in the portfolio into a meta-narrative of the increasing accessibility of the miraculously healthy apple that has contributed so much to humans though the centuries.

: : :

At around fifteen years many students will find that the growing amount of knowledge they have accumulated begins to require more complex modes of organizing and also, relatedly, more complex modes of sense making. The new tool kit that students develop in response to the array of knowledge contains prominently such learning tools as we have glanced at above, including the sense of abstract reality, the sense of agency, general theories and their anomalies, the search for authority and truth, and meta-narratives. These tools are related aspects of the abstract and theoretical world that often begins to be built in mid and later teen years. We may currently see clear evidence of this theoretic form of thinking in only a minority of students, but I suspect that is due to the fact that so many students learn too little knowledge to kick this process into action. I hope it will prove much more common if this project becomes widely implemented. I recognize that this section is more complex and abstract than the earlier sections. The kinds of thinking I have been describing, and the learning tools associated with those forms of thinking, are much less common in current forms of education. (For a more extended exposition of some of these ideas, see Egan 1997.)

Table 5.3 presents a summary of learning tools for the final years of schooling.

Table 5.3. Some prominent learning tools students in the final years of schooling can use in building their portfolios

Sense of abstract reality	The development of a theoretic world and organizing tools can be useful in further restructuring portfolios and adding new dimensions of interests and materials.
Sense of agency	Enables the students to extend the materials of their portfolios in the direction of social action and engagement. Their growing expertise can be seen as a source of influence in the everyday world around them.
General theories and their anomalies	This provides a mechanism for continued growth and development of portfolios through elaboration of their undergirding ideas and frameworks of organization.
The search for authority and Truth	Provides a goad to making their portfolios more reliable and reexamining and extending many dimensions that may have been relatively neglected for some years.
Meta-narratives	Drive the engagement of portfolio contents with powerful and emotional themes that shape the most general understanding of the topic.

Conclusion

What I have focused on in this chapter are some principles that might help teachers engage students' imaginations in their topics at different ages. I have chosen a set of strategies that are a little unusual, but no less effective for that. There are, of course, many other strategies that teachers can draw on to help students build their portfolios. Many excellent books and Web sites can give support to the somewhat new teaching task of encouraging this kind of learning in depth, including sites dedicated to providing support for teachers and also serving as repositories of ideas and experiences that teachers can share about supervising portfolios. They also provide forums for discussing a number of problems, difficulties, triumphs, techniques, examples, and so on that are involved in this new kind of teaching role.

Building the Portfolio

Maybe you think you now have a good enough sense of the LiD program and its potential value to students' education. No doubt, like me, you will have some doubts about how well it might be implemented, and some uncertainties about just how well such an ungraded addition to the curriculum, which relies on students' pleasure in learning, might actually work for many children. Especially when we look at average and below average performing students, we may be forgiven for wondering whether the basic human urge to learn will actually kick in on randomly assigned topics like *apples* or *beetles*. I have given a number of reasons to support the belief that, in the conditions of unforced learning that this project proposes, we will see unexpected engagement. Even if you are ready to go along with the possibility that it can all work out as suggested, you might still feel some vagueness about just what the project is going to look like in practice. Again, nothing like this has been tried before, and it is natural in such circumstances to ask for as clear a picture of what it will involve as possible.

So what will these portfolios look like? Where will students keep them? What will be the teacher's role exactly, and what will happen as students move from teacher to teacher? How different can portfolios be? What are student presentations going to be like, and what is their purpose?

What I would like to do in this chapter is try to give a sense of the project as it unfolds in everyday practice. I should add that this is my current image of how it might work, and I am well aware that others might be able to work out much better ways of implementing the LiD program, and, once we see it in practice in various schools, we will likely see revisions and more diverse and ingenious forms than the notions I currently have. (The Web sites associated with this book will also have pages in which we can gather "best practices" in implementing the basic idea.)

The Starting Ceremony

Students will be prepared for the ceremony by having it explained to them that during this event they will discover the topic about which they are going to become an expert: "At the end of this week we will have a very important day. It will be the day you will receive your 'special topic.' This will be something that will be uniquely yours: a topic that will grow, change, and flourish as much as you will throughout the years." This, it should be made clear, is no small matter, and is something that will effect their lives in a significant way. The ceremony itself should involve caregivers and teachers as well as the class of students, and perhaps others as I'll suggest below.

The student should be given some kind of container for the material they will begin to collect, perhaps a simple folder, which will be the beginning space for the portfolio. We need also to have something that the student can display to indicate the topic they have been given. If we use a folder we could include a sticker and a tile, both with the name of the topic written on them, the student's name, and a colored image of an apple, a beetle, a dust cloud, or whatever. The sticker could be put on the front of the folder, and the tile will become a part of a wall of such tiles in some prominent place in the school, where all students' tiles will be mounted. The student will announce, with appropriate help, the name of his or her topic to the assembled group.

One of the implementations currently underway used the following plan:

> After some careful thought, we are memorializing the topics on 2" academic medallions (on ribbons) that are inscribed with the topic and will be awarded to each student during the ceremony. We are also preparing a 1" three-ring binder that will serve as an organizing tool. It will be labeled with the student's name, the topic, and three "did you know" statements designed to get students thinking about their topics. (Robert Dunton, Corbett Charter School, Oregon)

After the program has been in operation for a few years, older students studying the same set of topics can present the folders to the grade 1 students. So Jake from a local high school might give Sara her topic of *apples*, and will be around to discuss it with her after the ceremony, and perhaps show Sara something of the portfolio he has developed so far; Ella from a nearby middle school can present Cloë with the topic *railways* and later show her some of her portfolio; and Nora from grade 3 in the same school can present the topic *camels* to Owen. Mingling the novices with older students who have been studying the topic for years, and with teachers, parents, and other caregivers can enrich the ceremony and its aftermath. This borrows an attractive feature from Waldorf schools, where senior students sometimes welcome newcomers with a flower.

Each school or school district might, of course, develop its own distinctive ceremony. I have recently heard about a school principal in Japan, who plans to implement the LiD program in his school, but the opening ceremony is going to involve giving each student the topic on a slip of paper inside a fortune cookie.

So the student's mind is alerted to whatever the topic is. The name creates a semantic space that the student is invited to begin the search for content to fill—a mini-version of the Big Bang that sets the cosmos going, accumulating material in the space it generates. That may not get the physics quite right, but I hope the image of creating cognitive expectations and a "space" to begin filling describes adequately one purpose for the ceremony. I am trying to emphasize the way in which we should prepare the students' minds for something out of the ordinary. This is an event they will remember, the moment at which an exploration of some consequence begins for each one of them. It would be desirable to have an occasion after the ceremony, perhaps over milk and cookies, during which the students have a chance to hear and talk about their topics with the adults and other students.

The Forms of Portfolios

Let us assume that we begin with the giving of a folder as the initial storage medium for the portfolio. After the ceremony each student will take her or his folder home. An identical folder will be provided, and this one will remain in the school with those of the other students. It will most conveniently be kept in the student's classroom, if no other dedicated space is available, such as a library. I imagine one of those expandable folders that have a set of dividers and one bigger space designed to hold the equivalent of a large format book.

The "home" folder can travel with the student, and its contents can be transferred to the school folder at regular intervals. For the first year it is likely that these folders will be sufficient. They will be filled with the basic information students can gather and maybe with the pictures students collect, their drawings and writing. The first contents will likely be equivalents of Sara's drawings of apples and her scoring system based on taste, along with lists of varieties. It might include some photographs that she, with a parent's help, has taken of different varieties of apple and apple trees. The emphasis in the early years should be on accumulating knowledge from what the student can experience, as far as possible—from what they can touch, see, and hear from others. Again, this needn't be exclusively the case, and other sources of knowledge can be used. I mention this just to make clear that there is no hurry to amass huge compilations of information in these early years.

The folders on *dust* and on *railways* or *beetles* will no doubt accumulate quite different contents. By grade 2 many folders will already be bulging, with, in the case of Nathan's *dust*, further drawings and photographs of dust mites and other miniature creatures found in dust, and on and on. A new folder, one with greater capacity and sections within it, is given to each student when the first becomes full. The further sections will require a new form of classifying the material already gathered and help develop relevant cognitive skills.

By the end of grade 2 or 3, some thought will need to be given to future forms for some portfolios. Many students will find the enlarged folder sufficient for some time, but in some cases models the student has made, or collections of *beetles* or whatever, will be added to the portfolios and some of these will be pushing the limits of physical portfolios. In such cases the class portfolio can contain pictures of large models or samples, and the artifacts can be stored elsewhere—at home if there is space, in some other dedicated place in the school if possible.

We will also want to encourage students to take stock of their portfolios at the beginning of each new school year. In some cases the reorganization of the topic might involve discarding some older material, but in some cases the topic growth may be more linear and cumulative. But a kind of meta-level reflection on the portfolio at least once each year is important.

By around grade 6, each student will be provided with space on a server to begin building an online digital dimension to his or her portfolio. This can help to solve some of the problems caused by excessive material in the physical portfolios; much of that material gathered so far can be scanned or put into some other digitized form and be added to the online part of the portfolio. Online development of the portfolio will need to begin slowly, and may be helped along by older mentors who have been working on the same topic. We don't want to have twenty or thirty children suddenly displacing their learning about *apples* or *birds*

with a need for intensive work learning about scanners and computers. Initially, we may expect the teacher to provide one or two
useful online sites, and recommend that students download one
new item for the portfolio and *do* something with it before insert-
ing it into the portfolio; they might, for instance, integrate some
information about the introduction of *apples* to the Americas with
the document in which they have been building a history of apple
varieties and their spread around the world.

The physical portfolio, though, will still be used for samples
and illustrations not easily put online. Indeed, it is possible that
some topics will not require computers and digitized online storage at all.

Students can begin to search out further material on the Internet if appropriate, gathering further information, and constructing, with teachers' help, categories to classify and reorganize their
accumulating store of knowledge. Sam, a student studying *beetles*,
for example, can begin to add information and even videos of
some of the more exotic and colorful beetles. For each addition,
though, the teacher's/supervisor's task is to ensure that Sam is not
simply accumulating "stuff" but is building knowledge and understanding, and he will be expected to show this by the way he
integrates new knowledge in meaningful ways with his growing
portfolio. One simple task at the end of each year would be to ask
the students to compose a list of ten "favorite" things discovered
during the year. Each year Sam and Sara and all the others will
be asked to revisit the ten items listed for each previous year, and
reconsider them, in an attempt to ensure that the contents of the
portfolio are constantly being reflected on, reassessed, manipu-
lated, reorganized—*thought about.*

For the next few years it is likely that the major growth in many
portfolios will be through online developments, though experiential exploration in most cases will continue to be significant and
should be encouraged. Quite quickly the general basic information—the kind one can find in encyclopedias, for example—will
be firmly in place, and sound organizational categories will be

established. Now Sam can begin exploring "records," such as the largest beetles, where one finds the most beetles, the smallest, the most colorful beetles, how much dung a dung beetle can process in a day, beetles in literature, flying beetles and record flights, beetles in songs, and so on. Sam's own interests should increasingly be the driver in these explorations, and teachers should feel it appropriate to encourage quite quirky pathways of inquiry: perhaps he will want to know how the bombardier beetles manage to produce an explosive puff of "smoke" from their rear, or why dung beetles spend so much time pushing around large balls of steer manure, or how the all-female small beetle called a Fuller's rose weevil manages; or perhaps he will collect photographs of decorations made from beetles' shells beginning with the stunning glimmering green hall ceiling of the Belgian royal palace, or begin construction of a beetle farm somewhere or at least begin a collection of beetle shells.

At grade 7 or 8, each student will be encouraged to enter the various online forums connected with their topic. So they will make contact with others who have the same topic through Wiki sites, Facebook-style networks, Web sites devoted to aspects of their topic, and whatever other community-of-knowledge formats may have been elaborated on the Internet. It seems possible that these will grow like *mushrooms* (another good topic!) once LiD programs get underway. Students' online portfolios can be synched with home computers and perhaps individual students' laptops, such that they can continue to add to their growing portfolios at almost any time. These portfolios can now begin to be linked to those of others, and individual quirky inquiries can be shared widely: those files on the history of dust, dust underwater, interplanetary dust, songs about dust, the spread of dust from volcanoes can become a part of the accessible database students can continue to explore.

There may be some call for Web sites in which students can share their knowledge and presentations—the idea of Di Fleming. Here are just a few of Di Fleming's suggestions:

- We could have online tutors who could support research on the LiD project. This would give us first hand knowledge of age/stage thinking/gender differences, and imaginative exploits.
- We could have an online LiD-KiDs' Stuff where students could store their research and exhibit their stories, cartoons, photos, poems, models, video blogs, wikis, images, drawings, etc.
- Kids could share with their friends, grandparents, teachers and the LiD team.
- Kids would have their own user names and passwords.
- Imagine in 20 years a LiDKiD writing a PhD on their LiDLife!
- LiDKiDs could provide a dynamic element to educational conferences, media, and publications as they build their own online portfolios.
- Second Life development around their topics could be wonderful—students could let their imaginations soar.

Discussions for the initial form of the site have brought forward many more ideas, and I suspect students attracted to such a site will elaborate on it in ways we can't now easily imagine.

It is, however, easy to imagine other possible scenarios, such as the following—to continue with our friend Sara:

Sara met Jon at a friend's party. They talked about their topics and decided that they should do a joint presentation at the end of the year. Jon's topic was *birds*, and they began work on a presentation that would show the many ways in which *apples* and *birds* interacted. Threading through their presentation was the Italian folk tale of the Singing Apple and the Talking Bird.

Jon's older cousin, it turned out, also had apples as a topic, and Jon invited Sara to meet him when he next visited. Sara took along an outline of her portfolio and the section on the historical development of apple species, of which she was most proud. Jon's cousin had his laptop with him and showed Sara a world map he had drawn that showed what species of apples were grown where and in what quantities. They discussed whether they might be able to merge the information they had and produce a similar map for every century from ancient Greek times till today.

Well, again, an idealized world may be a bit remote from most students' party activities today. But it is not implausible that a fairly wide implementation of LiD might create interactions among young people that are not currently normal.

Through the high school years both the online portfolio and the physical portfolios will continue to grow and change in structure. *Dust* for Nathan, like other topics for other students, will provide perspectives that begin to reshape his sense of the world in which he lives. The subject of his inquiries is in size about half way between a subatomic particle and the planet he lives on, it is made up from Nathan's, and everyone else's, skin, from decayed animal feces, from his clothes, from pollens, from minute life forms that thrive where we provide them with our organic material to feed on, and on and on. Nathan will become increasingly aware as his portfolio develops of the processes of life and of social and historical conditions that are interwoven with his topic. The world he sees will be different from the world you and I see, and the world each student will see will be different again as their topics enlarge their understanding. And their portfolios, most of which will be comprehensive, huge, and well organized, will support that understanding. Each student will have a space in school and at home where they keep a physical portfolio about their topic. For many students, the bulk of their portfolio will be on a server kept by the school district, and backed up on their own computers. I suspect, in most cases, the end of schooling will not be the end of their additions to their portfolios.

Portfolio Supervision

Who is to do the supervision? Should the school try to ensure the same teacher stays with a group of children for their LiD program as long as possible, or should it be the job of the classroom teacher and change each year? Should special LiD supervising teachers be hired? Does it have to be a teacher—or could someone less qualified handle the job? How would the supervisor interact with all those others mentioned as helping students, such as librarians, parents, older students, college students, and others? And what knowledge or skills does a teacher need to have to be able to do the job most effectively?

Let us begin at the beginning. It would seem desirable that teachers or others who will be supervising portfolio development with a group of students should obviously need to understand the aims of the program. The program itself is not complicated, but it is desirable that any prospective supervisors should take at least a two-day workshop that will familiarize them with the aims and also give them guidance in how to engage students in topics and support them as the program goes forward.

To back up the workshop, the supervising teachers should also be given two kinds of written supports, which can be supplemented by further materials made available through LiD Web sites. The first kind of support will be some basic information about each of the topics they are to supervise, and this information will need to be suitable for the age of the students with whom they will be working. A booklet might also include suggestions for activities the students can become involved in that will engage their minds in exploring their topics. Producing this kind of support will take some time, but I think it will accumulate quickly with the help of teachers and LiD researchers. (Two are available—on apples and money—on the main LiD Web site.)

The second kind of support that should be made available is suggestions about how to engage the imaginations of students at specific ages with the topics. That is, the focus here is on students' minds and what most readily will attract them to inquire about their topics energetically.

The first kind of support can be provided in a basic way by whoever is organizing the program in a school or a school district. In the first instance, the LiD Web sites will provide information on each of the topics it recommends as appropriate, beginning with the set at the end of chapter 4, and information on these can be downloaded to provide a basic starting point for the supervising teachers, acknowledging that many teachers will not want or need such prepared material and will prefer to find their own or rely on their own knowledge base and teacherly skills. Such information can be augmented by some further research by organizers of the program within school districts. Teachers will, of course, likely find extra material on some of the topics they will supervise. As time goes by, their knowledge about most of the topics they supervise will grow and can be added to whatever is available on the LiD Web sites. Teachers can also contribute to the Web sites ideas about activities that work especially well, so we will develop a resource of "best practices" expertise.

The second kind of support may be rather like a version of the suggestions in the previous chapter. These can be organized into a form better suited for a handout to be given to supervisors. Again, experience and teachers' own suggestions might enrich this support, and Web sites will provide a means for supervising teachers' experience to be made available to others. That is, both kinds of support—of the background information that will supply initial avenues for students to explore and of the strategies that can engage students' imaginations in their topics—can quickly be elaborated through Wiki pages on LiD Web sites.

Initially I assumed that the regular classroom teacher would always be the student's portfolio supervisor, but a number of teachers have argued that it would work better if the student kept with the same supervising teacher for a number of years, as long as the students were in the same school. I can see how it would be easier to organize supervision if the regular classroom teacher handles it, but I am certainly open to the alternative suggested. The reason why I suspect the supervisor can change relatively painlessly in this program is that after a very short time, the students will know more about their topics than any teacher. The supervisor's role is less a direct teaching role and more a support role, helping with suggestions, guiding questions, recommendations for avenues worth exploring, and so on. And we do assume that changing the teacher each year will be no problem for the regular curriculum.

While it may work to hire people other than regular teachers to supervise portfolios, I suspect the skills teachers acquire over their training and years of experience will be important to making this program a success. Parent volunteers, older students, and librarians can all help to reduce the time burden on the teacher supervisor, but I think the students' portfolio development needs generally to be guided by teachers' skill and experience. These concerns seem important especially during the first three years of students' work on their topics, but thereafter I imagine most students will become year by year increasingly independent, needing to check in with their supervisors only for feedback and occasional suggestions. No doubt this will not be true of all students, and some may forever need a bit of prodding and more active guidance than most. But even in these cases, the Wiki sections of the LiD Web site should be useful as a repository of suggestions about how to help the more needy students sustain engagement with their topics.

Presentations and Their Purposes

The presentation is an opportunity for students to share the results of their work and receive feedback on it from their peers and from others, including parents, teachers, and older and younger students. The presentation is also a moment of pause and public celebration in what will be largely a private activity of developing a portfolio. That is, even while students begin to make contact with others studying the same topic, and discussing with others how they might combine features of their topics, their own portfolio is uniquely theirs and will grow and change under the direction of their interests and inquiries.

Presentations can be scheduled once a year and can take many forms. Individual students may want to make a brief presentation on some feature of their work that they have found most interesting during the previous year, or they may choose to make a joint presentation with one or two or a number of friends with different topics about which a coherent presentation can be structured. Within a short time, I am sure, the routine and conventional presentation, with perhaps an overhead projector, will soon give way to more adventurous formats, in which performance, multimedia, artwork, and music will begin to come into play.

One aim of the presentation is increased student confidence and skill at speaking to an audience. A basic aim of the program is to give students confidence through knowing something, and that confidence will be enlarged if we encourage development of other skills as they learn.

The celebratory function of presentations is also important. Some mark of achievement helps others to see the growing expertise of the student, and helps the student recognize the progress he or she is making. These presentations could be available throughout the year, and could thus become a new aspect of the school's activity. The degree to which these should be open sessions, available to all who want to come, should be determined by the teachers and the norms of the school, informed somewhat by each student's own wishes. Maybe for the first three or four years, the presentations might best be restricted to the class group, with occasional others invited by the student. But as the students become older they should be encouraged to address their presentations to wider audiences. A digital video recording of the presentations can become a part of students' portfolios.

The logistics of presentations should not be ignored, of course. If each student in a school will be making a presentation once a year, that will mean some space and time will be needed on a very frequent basis for this activity. It may be that two or more presentations might have to be made at the same time in different rooms. I think there are many ways this can be dealt with: for example, the school might organize conference-style presentations, restricted to specific days, perhaps once per semester, with multiple parallel presentations available for the audience to choose among at any one time. I can imagine schools finding varied ways of managing this.

Student Differences

What are we to do about differences in students' ability and achievement in compiling a portfolio? Some students will have supportive and sensitive parents helping them and learning along with them, but not interfering inappropriately in what is the students' project. Other students will not have such good fortune; they may have parents or caregivers who have little interest in the students' LiD work or may, on the other hand, have intrusive parents who want to constantly shape the portfolio according to their own preferences, unaware perhaps of how they are taking over their child's task. Some students will have easy access to computers and may have their own laptops from an early age; others may have more difficult access and little support. What are we to do about these inequities?

One of the criteria for identifying suitable topics for the LiD program was that topics should be able, as far as possible, to provide students with equally rich experiences as they explore them. But should we also try to ensure equal outcomes, similarly rich portfolios at the end of the program for each student? Is this a program in which elitism or egalitarianism is to thrive?

My hope is that it will be a program in which great diversity will be allowed to thrive, without comparisons on some artificial and inappropriate criterion of "rightness" for portfolios.

In general, the portfolios are to be free from assessment and are to be constructed by the student according to the student's interests. Will this not lead to unequal results, such that some portfolios will be massive, complex, and enormously enriching to the students who compose them, while others will look in comparison dull, uninteresting, and not at all complex? I think the problem words there are "in comparison." Who will be doing the comparing? No doubt the students themselves will be doing so, but my suspicion is that even the duller portfolios will be, in comparison to typical projects students may do in school today, hugely more accomplished. Also, each student will increasingly be tied in with networks of others, sharing ideas, findings, and suggestions, but, always, some more and some less than others.

The uncommitted students, who may lack the kind of energy and engagement of many of their peers, will, even so, be putting together something on a scale and complexity beyond anything they are challenged to do today. The interactions students will have with others working on the same topic, and the easy ability to transfer components of portfolios, especially from Wiki sites, will likely mean that most portfolios will look formidably complex, and it would only be by looking carefully and at length that the richer and more complex portfolios would be evident to an observer.

Well, that's the weasel response to the question. Will some portfolios be obviously hugely better than others? Of course. What should we do about it? Nothing; absolutely nothing. We should simply help and encourage each student put together the kind of portfolio she or he is drawn to construct.

We have created an educational system in which nearly all formal learning is forced in some way. Nearly all formal learning is subject to assessment, because we tend to assume that students need to be "motivated" to learn. That is, we have created a system in which the kind of easy, "natural" learning of the streets and fields that John Dewey wanted to see brought into schools is not generally expected to happen. Our system is based on the belief that we cannot give students a choice about whether they should learn, say, algebra or not, because we fear the results, and it is clearly believed that to "motivate" them to learn algebra we need to assess them and allot benefits in school and in life in proportion to how well they manage.

The LiD program is based on the belief that students' learning when unassessed and uncoerced will likely produce results quite different from what we consider inevitable in our current schools. These likely different results are a product of removing the program from the commitment of the schools to produce required learning for various social purposes and from the consequent

need to assess students to help determine their future social roles
and jobs.

Some of the schools' difficulties in achieving easy and widespread learning are tied to its role as a crucial social agency delivering skills suitable for democratic social life and a national
economy. By setting itself outside of these commitments, the LiD
program has a chance at achieving a kind of learning that is currently rare within our school systems—though far from rare in
our experience outside schools' demands (think again of those
hobbies and collections, that local Civil War buff, the surprising
expertise built up by an aunt about eighteenth-century manners,
and so on.) A corollary of this is that the quality of students' portfolios are to play no part in their selection for particular jobs—the
portfolio is not an item to be placed on one's résumé—nor is it to
be a component to be used in deciding on university placement,
and so on. Now I recognize that this is a somewhat idealistic, not
to say unrealistic, expectation. After working so hard for so long
and accumulating so much knowledge and understanding, can't
one use it for some more utilitarian purpose? No doubt one can't
stop that from happening to some degree. I would only warn that
every utilitarian use of the portfolio is a diminishment of what it
can best do for the student.

Well, that has taken us some way from the issue of what we are
to do about the fact that some portfolios will be much better than
others. But, of course, it is far from a simple issue. About some
features of human differences, we can do nothing. But what can
we do about the cruder differences in access to knowledge among
students? Some students will be in schools with few computers
and restricted access to them, and in homes with little interest in
accumulating "useless" knowledge. I suspect this will increasingly
be less of a problem in the future, as access to the Internet will
become less a matter of economic power and more a public right.
But it is important to remember that much of the work of building a portfolio is not going to be simply a matter of downloading
information. It will be at least as much about studying species
of beetle or samples of dust, seeking out and tasting varieties of

apples, measuring railway lines and counting railway ties, and *exploring topics by means of experience in the world*. Also there are grounds to propose that LiD portfolios should use the Internet in only very restricted ways for the first five or six years, as I argued earlier.

And what are we to do about the student who says, after six months or a year or two or ten years, that they are fed up with their topic and don't want to continue with their portfolios? Nothing; absolutely nothing. Let them stop. My expectation, especially in the early years, is that after a period of relief the dropouts will face an environment in which most of their peers are becoming both expert and engaged by their developing portfolios. Dropouts can be told that they can begin again any time they want, maybe months later or a year or more later. In some cases it may be that it is something about the topic that has turned them off, in which case they can be given a new topic. Some students will drop out and stay out. Nothing is lost from the school's point of view—the school will simply have a student doing much the same as all students do today. I suspect this will be rarer than many people might predict, but only experience will tell. (When administrators or teachers in a school raise this as a potential problem—some predicting massive dropout rates within the first few years—I say that I will give them $20 for every student who wants to drop out. But the deal is that they give me $20 for every student who continues.)

I do fear that the already discouraged students might drop out most readily, and in some poor schools, that might become the fashionable option. This might lead to a situation in which nearly all students in "good" schools do LiD and nearly all students in poor schools don't. Being alert to the possibility might enable us to be somewhat forearmed, by concluding that the resources and support for students in poor schools need to be greater. How we are to ensure that I don't know. But an administrator who might hope to boost some engagement by students in what has been an underperforming school needs to be aware that the LiD program is not going to take off without some considerable planning and effort. On the other hand, an active LiD program can be a catalyst in boosting school performance in general.

: : :

No doubt as LiD programs get underway, they will take on forms I am not able to imagine. There is something odd about trying to describe practical details for a program that has so far only a few pilot programs underway. And no doubt the early experiences with the program will answer in a much more clear way many of the questions I have hesitantly tried to respond to in this chapter. The results of the pilot programs, and support for anyone who wants to begin such a program, will be available on the LiD Web site at www.ierg.net/LiD.

Another obvious feature of these LiD programs that I have not explored, because I cannot, is that different schools' values and mission statements will influence the way LiD is implemented. There are various ways LiD can be structured and practiced, reflecting and coordinating with the unique characteristics of particular schools. While one aim of the LiD program is to achieve a transformation of the experience of schooling for students, the program itself is not supposed to direct or change much of the school's everyday activities. Each school, with its professional community, is obviously in the best position to determine how the program can fit into its school culture and organization. Nor should we expect that some precise and regular implementation process can be instituted for all schools wanting to try LiD. The program will take on a life of its own as teachers and administrators fit it to their own educational context. What I am trying to do here is lay out what seems to me a basic set of principles that can be adopted and adapted by individual schools, which, in the end, Sinatra-like, will do it their way.

What Do We Do Next? **7**

What we do next, if persuaded that this idea is worth trying, will depend on who "we" are, of course. If "we" are me, I'm largely done by writing this book, though I will be active on the Learning in Depth project Web sites and in promoting the idea by giving talks and supporting research on pilot projects. But if "we" are teachers or parents who find this idea attractive, then certain steps suggest themselves. If "we" are school district administrators, then other steps are available. If "we" are faculty in schools or colleges of education, then another set of steps is appropriate. And if "we" are the emperor/empress of the educational galaxy, well, instructions to put it all into place tomorrow will be fine.

What, then, if "we" are parents, teachers, school administrators, department of education officials, or instructors and professors in teacher education programs? Let's take each group one at a time and see how someone in that role might help bring this proposal into being. I feel a bit silly writing this chapter, recognizing that making such suggestions smacks not a little of megalomania: Why expect anyone to be faintly interested in this project, and how dare I assume it will become something many people might want to support?

No defense, guilty as charged; but so many people have been engaged by the idea after the first descriptions of it appeared that it doesn't seem entirely daft to give some advice in print of the kind I have been asked for in "real life." I also feel a bit silly because many of the people I am addressing will have a far better idea than I have about what they might be able to do to bring this project toward implementation. The only defense here is that these suggestions come after discussions with people in each of the categories mentioned below, and may be of some help.

Parents

Parents often don't recognize how powerful they are with regard to schools, as they are occasionally awed by various official groups' claims to expertise, assertions of authority, and claims that "the research shows" x or y. But they, as citizens, ultimately support the whole system via taxes or more direct payments, and they supply the students that make the whole thing turn over. If particular parents like the idea of Learning in Depth, they can begin by bringing it to the attention of teachers or school board officials. Either they could simply describe the idea and/or refer them to the Learning in Depth project Web pages or parents could give a copy of the introduction to the project that is available as Appendix B of this book and also is available in downloadable form from the LiD Project Web pages.

This project seems to have a number of potential benefits to parents. One concerns simply the degree of interest their children will find in schooling; I anticipate that for many children this will increase significantly. (Even as a result of the first year of an implementation for grade 3 students, one parent said to the teacher that this was the first time their son had come home and energetically told them about what he was learning.)

Another advantage should be the development of a real and specific interest in something quite removed from their everyday world. And what's the advantage of that? Well, it begins the great adventure that human beings as a species embarked on millennia ago—the accumulation of detailed and expert knowledge, which gives a distinctive kind of pleasure. It also takes the focus of their minds away from themselves and their everyday world.

I recognize these likely advantages might seem the result of excessive optimism, and unreality, on my part. Realistic people will suggest that this vision of little scholars all over the place ignores the realities of the iPod- and TV-saturated world of pop culture. But that world is a product of a weakness in our current educational system that this proposal is designed to fix, or at least contribute toward fixing. I recognize, too, that suggesting taking students' minds from their everyday world seems to contradict a central assumption of how children learn—but I have given reasons why we might doubt that assumption above, and in other books (e.g., Egan 1997, 2002).

If we take this project seriously, we should expect some significant differences in our schools. I think the above two are prominent among the benefits that might follow from implementing this proposal. Parents might imagine the change that could occur if they help their children in building these new kinds of portfolios. So the third thing parents can do is imagine the curious pleasure they might have in exploring along with their children something new and extensive. If parents describe to teachers or other educational officials how they might enjoy supporting their children's portfolio building, this would help people within the education system to think more favorably about the possibility and potential attractiveness of implementing this project.

If more than one parent in an area becomes interested in this proposal, they can begin to solicit interest among other parents whose children might attend the same school. After a meeting at someone's house, perhaps, at which parents might share their ideas about the project, and consider its advantages in their own school, they could compose a list of what they see as the advantages such a project might bring to the schooling experience of their children. Those parents could then ask school officials to provide space and time for a meeting about the applicability of the project in their schools, inviting the officials and teachers to attend. This is to imagine energetic, committed, and likely wealthy parents with free time for such activities. But any parent who hears about the project, and likes what seem to be its possible benefits for their child or children, can mention it to teachers, or indicate they would like to know more about its possibilities for their school.

If the parents feel that this project is workable, they might even ask to give a presentation about it to a meeting of their school board. The LiD Web site contains materials that might enable them to make an effective presentation, including Keynote and PowerPoint presentations. (One school that was interested in a hesitant way in implementing LiD asked the LiD team to address the parents. It was by far the most appreciative and enthusiastic audience we have had. Administrators and teachers immediately focus on the problems of implementation, whereas the parents focused only on the educational value to their children. One parent's response after the talk and discussion was to ask the senior administrators why they hadn't already implemented LiD rather than just talk about it! Well, the administrators were being appropriately cautious because they had to face the detailed problems of how to manage an addition to the school's work.)

Teachers

What can a teacher who is attracted by the possibilities of this project do? Individual teachers can, of course, implement it by themselves in their own classrooms, as some have already done. It works better, of course, if there is a commitment by a whole school, and better yet if there is support from a school district. This wouldn't mean that all schools and teachers in a district would need to take part, but that some district support would make it easier for any implementation to take place. The program could be managed in an individual school, of course, and that's the first arena any teacher can work in. Private schools, of course, can much more easily implement it within a single school without having to deal with public authorities who always have to look over their shoulders to what they assume are the political forces within which they can operate. Within a school, a start can be made when a teacher gives a professional development (Pro-D) day presentation about the project to her or his colleagues. Again, materials to help with such a presentation are available on the LiD Web sites and in a LiD Support Materials kit available from ierg-ed@sfu.ca.

From a number of comments I have made so far it will be obvious that, since I began writing this book, a number of individual teachers have begun to implement the idea in their own classrooms, occasionally enlisting one or two colleagues as well. I had initially assumed that implementation would require the usual difficulties of negotiating with various authorities before being allowed to give it a try. I had underestimated the initiative and enthusiasm of many teachers.

If two or more teachers find the idea attractive, they might discuss how best they can spread information about it to their colleagues, in a more sustained way than they can at a single Pro-D presentation. They might ask their principal to arrange a talk about the project, to be given by them or by an outside expert. They say an expert is someone who comes from a long distance with a briefcase. Such people are available! Sometimes an outsider can be effective in supporting the work of the teachers on-site, and tying them into a wider network of those interested in implementing the project.

Though nearly everything written in this book has been aimed at a relatively wide implementation of the project, it is worth bearing in mind that one or two schools can implement it themselves. It would need coordination between an initiating K–7 school and the school or schools to which most of the students would then continue.

Teachers also have considerable influence on school boards and can express that influence by advocacy addressed to particular school board members they might know or, more formally if the occasion arises, joining with parent groups to advocate the project's adoption either within an individual school, a set of schools, or within some larger organizational grouping.

Teachers who might be taking college or university courses can, of course, use such opportunities to learn more about it, and also to promote the idea in their classes. By writing papers about it they can clarify for themselves their own thinking, explore how they might better implement it in their own classes, and at the same time spread information and ideas about it to others, including their instructors. They can also write about it for teachers' magazines and journals.

Teachers can try to find and take college or university courses or workshops that prepare them to be effective in supporting students in Learning in Depth programs. While the general notion of helping students explore particular topics may seem straightforward, some further expertise about how to do it best should come in handy. Also a deeper understanding about the aims of the program in general would no doubt help them to be stronger advocates for the program and also more effective portfolio supervisors. The kind of information given in the previous chapter, elaborated and with opportunities for practice, would also be useful. Like most things to do with schooling, if the teachers are not comfortable with the idea and prepared to apply appropriate skills to making it work, the results are likely to be disappointing.

For all the above activities teachers can find supporting information and materials on the LiD Web sites.

School Principals and Vice-Principals

Though I have focused on system-wide change, indeed, galaxy-wide change, it is possible to have this project implemented in a single classroom or in a single K–7 school. I mentioned earlier that one might need to have arrangements made for the students to continue their projects in the next year's classroom or in high schools. One teacher who began a single-year implementation, thinking he could make it a feature of his rather unusual class each year (made up largely of "at-risk" students, some labeled "gifted," some "disadvantaged") has had to scramble as the end of the year approached to make arrangements with their next year's teacher to enable the students to continue with their portfolios—at the students' insistence. The support of an appreciative vice-principal made it all work more smoothly.

An interested principal and vice-principal, whose teaching staff is on-side, could indeed implement the project in a single school. The LiD Web sites, again, will support such implementations with materials and advice. It will also provide a forum for school officials to discuss among themselves their problems and solutions. We also have available a live video-supported resource pack.

Committed school principals can, of course, promote the idea among their peers, making reference to the Web sites or passing around relevant literature about the project, beginning by handing out copies of the brief outline in Appendix B and on the Web sites. They can also give talks to their peers at meetings and conferences, especially if they have begun to implement the project in their own school. All groups are more influenced by their peers than by "outside" advocates. Even so, principals who would like to see the project made known to colleagues might also request the briefcased expert from far away to come and add her or his insights and enthusiasm.

School administrators are usually very busy people, and if they are supportive of the idea, it may be that their best support might be to designate someone in the school staff to spearhead the LiD work.

School District Officials

If this project is to become more than a boutique activity pursued in a minor way by occasional schools or individual classes, it must attract the interest of those who frame policy in school districts. These decision makers are far from immune to persuasion by others in the system, but, in the end, they have to set in motion the actions that will lead to significant implementation.

They can decide that it won't fly, is too expensive, is too disruptive of other school activities, is ideologically objectionable, or any of an unpredictable range of reasons to stop it dead in any particular school district. They may, alternatively, decide it has sufficient promise, and support from some principals and teachers, that they will authorize a limited pilot project in a few schools for a limited time—say, three or five years. Or they may be so convinced that implementing this project can indeed transform the experience of schooling in desirable ways that they authorize a widespread implementation and the resources necessary to adequately support it.

Of these three possibilities, I hope the first will not be the commonest response. I suspect the third will be rare for some time, and I suspect the second—limited pilot projects—may be common.

Instructors in Colleges and Universities

This section ought to be easiest to write, as this is my job. If this project is to become adequately implemented, then support for it needs to be made available in teacher preservice and in-service professional programs. So people who work in such institutions can design and propose courses or segments of courses to prepare teachers for this curriculum innovation.

Professors wishing to support implementation of this project can also propose conference presentations, to spread the idea among their peers. Papers could explore the theory behind the idea or consider ways to improve parts of the project as described here. Implementations in single schools or school districts could also provide a focus for research and future publications. Conference presentations can also be reworked after responses from colleagues and be submitted for journal publication.

If three or more faculty members in an institution are interested in exploring the idea further, and might find it helpful to discuss it with colleagues from other institutions, and engage interested teachers, they could organize a small conference.

One or more professors, locally or from different countries, could propose a research project shaped around some of the potential problems or questions raised by implementing LiD. There is no shortage of issues that could do with study, and careful research can involve professors and their graduate students in generating knowledge about what are major problems with the proposal as it stands, what can work, what might be better done, and so on.

They could also contact the LiD Web site and sign up as members, helping to promote the ideas. They could offer workshops at teacher Pro-D days, both describing the project and how teachers can become involved in implementing it.

Emperor/Empress of the Educational Galaxy

A problem for achieving any educational change is to work out who can actually make something happen. The administrative machinery involved in bringing about such a curriculum innovation is immensely complicated. Even if many parents, teachers, school principals, lecturers, professors, school district officials, and others were in favor of implementing this project, what would it take to bring it into reality? Who has to do what, even after all the people mentioned above engage in advocacy on behalf of it? I am not entirely clear. But if the emperor/empress of the educational galaxy is out there, please contact the LiD Web site.

We have many books about the implementation process in schools, and they ought to offer some help to a project like this. But it is hard to find anything addressed to a curriculum innovation of quite this kind, and so there may be unexpected problems or possibilities that only trials and practice will bring out. Indeed, a slight oddity of looking through books on implementation and "change" (why not "improvement"?) in schools is that no one seems to imagine a new component for the curriculum. The books seem to be largely obsessed with how to improve test scores, how to manage assessment and accountability systems, or how to control teachers and teaching more reliably and predictably. These focuses are the result of trying to address the problem I began with: the perceived inadequacy of students' knowledge when they leave school. But in response to systems that have become increasingly driven by assessment, which have had questionable effects, except in boosting for a while the test scores of the less able students (thus giving a disproportionate-seeming boost to overall scores), it is as though their proponents can think only of offering more of the same. They draw a lot on the business world for ideas and practices. Unquestionably, attention to such books can help us avoid some of the more common pitfalls of innovations in schooling.

:::

It does, however, seem that if the above groups begin to make their voices known and take the initiatives that are within their range of action, then we may see quite rapid uptake of the project. There are emperors/empresses of particular schools, as mentioned above. That is, there are people whose agreement can enable implementation of LiD in a particular school. There are larger scale empresses/emperors whose concerted action can ensure its implementation in a number of schools in particular school districts. Maybe that is the way it can happen. We may see small-scale implementations that seem to work well enough, without causing large-scale problems, and then others being sufficiently impressed to try it themselves. Research studies will help to sort out what works and what is problematic, allowing refinement of the program. News of beneficial results will spread quickly. Regional implementation might then follow, and tomorrow the galaxy.

As with most things, the first steps are likely to be the hardest. If we imagine a first implementation in a school, we would need to have enthusiastic administrators and full buy-in from the teachers. Not easy, but far from impossible. What we need to do next, then, is locate schools whose administrators and teachers are sufficiently persuaded that this might deliver significant benefits and who are willing to give it a try.

I do recognize that writing as though everyone in the educational galaxy may be champing at the bit to implement LiD is more than a bit odd. Most people are totally unaware of it. But this chapter was intended to make some suggestions for action that respond to questions I have been asked by people at various places in the educational system.

Our Web site, http://www.ierg.net/LiD/, contains much more information on the practicalities of implementing Learning in Depth. Please visit the site to see how to get started, to download additional classroom materials, and join in discussions of some of the experiences of schools that have already started LiD.

Conclusion

I think people who have only the sketchiest sense of knowledge, because they know nothing in depth, easily confuse their wishes, needs, and opinions with knowledge, and in so doing create many of our most serious social and political problems. They also have only the most tenuous ability to develop flexible imaginations, and they accept crude fantasies as readily as or more readily than they accept reality. These are social and political pathologies that will be devastated by widespread implementation of this project. (Maybe this might seem evidence of my crude fantasy, but I think it is rather better based!)

You can imagine how Sara, Nathan, and Sam at the end of their schooling will have immensely stimulating material that can engage and enrich their imaginations when it comes to thinking about *apples, dust,* and *beetles,* and things related to them. Without serious and significant knowledge, the imagination cannot do its best work. What do the silver apples of the moon, the golden apples of the sun, call up in your mind and emotions? To Sara they spark a vast array of images, knowledge, stories, flavors, mysteries, and delight about apples stretching back through precise history, tangled with roses. And Nathan walks though a world of dust, recognizing it almost as a friend. When he hears the words "and to dust thou shalt return," he sees not simple decay because he knows that the return to dust is part of vast cycles of life, in which the earth too will disintegrate and become material for new stars and planets and forms of life. That dust in the corner of the room is to him full of wonder. And Sam is an expert on beetles who is fascinated by their immense variety of species. That beetle we might both see with small curiosity is to Sam an intricately known miracle. They are all amateurs, in its original sense—doing something for the love of it. Their knowledge has *not* been built over the years while overcoming a series of assessment hurdles and preparing for a thicket of exams. It has not been tied up with their ambitions for certain jobs or awards

I recognize that this book may seem to present a neat and tricky addition to the curriculum that just might work to help students learn a great deal about something in particular, but that it has a very limited educational aim, narrow and impoverished in scope compared to the social and even moral purposes that education is also about. I think this view would be mistaken. Learning about the world, when done properly, is not merely an accumulation of bits of knowledge, like collecting hockey or football statistics. It would perhaps be excessive to call up Plato and St. Francis of Assisi as support for the potential wider value of what can happen to a student who becomes involved in learning something in depth. But both Plato and St. Francis point out that a central feature of becoming a moral person is to learn to become engaged with something outside the self, rather than seeing the world only in terms of one's self and one's needs. The LiD project, apart from the more straightforward educational values I have discussed so far, also encourages students to lose themselves in something outside themselves. It is a multiyear training in attending to something distinct—to learning the virtues of accuracy, precision, and also a respect for truth. I think is would be a mistake to ignore this potential value of the program.

: : :

You can, of course, individually, start your own LiD project at any time. Maybe look at the table of topics at the end of chapter 5, close your eyes, and begin on whatever you touch down on, today.

Appendix A

Foundations for Learning in Depth

Having read this far, you are likely, I hope, to be taking the idea seriously, but you may reasonably be asking where the idea comes from, in the sense of what are its genesis and foundations, in order to get some handle on how it sticks to the more familiar world of educational ideas, research, and practices. As the book stands so far, it is sort of hanging in midair, supported by something that isn't very clear. So far perhaps we lack intellectual scenery into which this idea can fit with any comfort. That's what I have provided in this appendix. This appendix is here in response to requests by some kind readers of the manuscript who asked for something more in the way of support for the idea. This lengthy appendix is for the hardy of soul and constitution who are ready to take on a hacking trek through a thicket of educational ideas.

I hope I may be forgiven if I work my way into this via some book-autobiography, or autobibliography I suppose. A few years ago I published a book called *The Educated Mind: How Cognitive Tools Shape Our Understanding* (1997.) The book did fairly well, as education books go, and has been translated, or is in process of translation, into about a dozen other languages. But it was a book I didn't finish. It had taken a long time to research and write. It laid out an alternative theory of education to those currently on offer, and that theory led to somewhat changed conceptions of teaching, the curriculum, and the school. Having described the general theory, I then launched into its implications for teaching and the curriculum—to show, at least, that the kind of teaching and curriculum that were implied or entailed by this new theory were not weird or exotic, and indeed might resonate better with what most people feel education ought to be like than do current general schemes and our school culture. I then turned to writing the final chapter, on the implications for the school. I amassed my texts, which stood in vertiginous piles on my desk, and lost heart. I didn't have the energy. And the scale of the task was so great that I couldn't see how I could compress it into a single chapter. So the book was published without the implications for the nature of the school.

A while later I sat down to write that planned final chapter as a separate book. I had decided to begin by dealing with the founding of the public schools in the mid-nineteenth century and to excavate the ideas that gave shape to the schools we have. I thought this a useful approach because many people take what currently exists as somehow firm and fixed and almost unquestionable, almost as natural, so that any alternative is interrogated in a fierce way and condemned to the degree that it isn't like what currently exists. As I wanted to suggest something new, it seemed a good strategy to show how the forms of education that currently exist, which many take for granted, were and are a product of a set of ideas that are at least as dodgy as anything I was proposing.

This approach required a close reading of Herbert Spencer's voluminous works, and I became increasingly convinced of Spencer's enormous influence on our schools and on the curriculum that currently exists within them. His brief book about education (*Education: Intellectual, Moral, and Physical*) was first published in New York in 1859, and in London the following year, and went through dozens of printings from various publishers in the latter half of the nineteenth century, and hundreds of thousands of copies were sold in the United States alone. Why, I wondered, was he now almost forgotten in education—except for the occasional reminder by someone of the title of one of the four essays that constituted his book: "What Knowledge Is of Most Worth?" The more I read, the more I became interested in Spencer's strange life, and in Beatrice Webb's account of it in her wonderful *My Apprenticeship* (1926). Spencer's apparently far-right-wing agenda of social Darwinism (though this popular view is also simplistic and misleading [Gay 1998; Francis 2007]) created something of a dilemma for the socialist John Dewey and the generally left-inclined people who framed the school system, so Spencer's name tended to disappear, even when such monumental institutional effects as the 1918 Commission on the Reorganization of Secondary Education are almost a direct translation of Spencer's ideas (Egan 2002, chap. 4; Lawrence Cremin wrote about the commission and its results that "most of the important and influential movements in the field since 1918 have simply been footnotes to the classic itself" [1955, p. 307], and Tanner and Tanner state, "Its impact on educational policy has yet to be equaled" [1980, p. 275]).

Well, the problem here was that the book I was trying to write about the school was already becoming deformed, and as I continued to explore Spencer's barely acknowledged influence in the making of modern school, I became increasingly concerned that this book, too, would never end. So, surgery was performed, and the main part of the book was cut away for future attention, and I made a separate book, which was published with the cheerful title *Getting It Wrong from the Beginning: Our Progressivist Inheritance from Herbert Spencer, John Dewey, and Jean Piaget* (2002).

But I *still* hadn't finished the final chapter I had planned for *The Educated Mind*. I turned back to the draft material that was excised from the 2002 book and began to work it into a third book. The opening part went fairly straightforwardly, as it was mainly an elaboration of earlier work, but, by a moderately cruel irony, the latter two-thirds of the book coincided with my having to found and direct the organization whose fictionalized future I was also writing about. Setting up the Imaginative Education Research

Group (http://www.ierg.net) slowed down writing the book, as I snatched time between meetings, writing Web page material, giving talks, dealing with personnel issues, etc. The book was eventually published as *The Future of Education: Reimagining Our Schools from the Ground Up* (2008). The latter part of the book purports to describe the "history" of education from 2010 to 2060, as written by a historian far in the future. Instead of writing a utopian account of how schooling might be better, I tried to show how it might plausibly change step by step from current conditions to those characterized in *The Educated Mind*, so finishing the final "chapter" of that book. In fact, 95 percent of that "future history" is nothing other than an account of how the ideas in the earlier part of the book can be put into practice, with a discussion of the implications of that practice for schooling. I could have written it straightforwardly as a section on implications for the school, but thought the rhetorical 5 percent would make it more engaging to read.

And where does LiD fit into all that? Well, LiD made its first appearance as one of the practices of schooling that were projected to be common by 2030. In order to show why it is an appropriate part of future schooling, I need to address the conception of education that supports it.

When I have described LiD, either in talks or short articles, the response has usually been—shall we say?—energetic. On the one hand, there is often enthusiastic support and an expressed desire to start implementing it tomorrow, and sometimes there is angry dismissal of the idea as utterly idiotic, and, I should acknowledge, mostly there are just reasonable expressions of doubt and caution. I tried in chapter 3 to describe and respond to some of the hostile objections the idea receives or I imagine it could receive. Why does it sometimes hit such a raw nerve, and what makes some people so enthusiastic? Well, that brings us to the complicated theoretical issue that continues, as it has continued since the founding of the public schools, to divide people about education today.

Knowledge and Mind

In chapter 3 I tried to deflect the question about what research support there is for this program. That is the usual question we raise about any new proposal in education. I argued there that the general question about whether we should introduce this new curriculum element is a matter of values and meanings—asking for evidence that it should be introduced to the curriculum is like asking for evidence to support continuing to teach the social studies.

This is, as it were, the negative argument. LiD is more like social studies than like some new empirically testable technique of teaching that we hope to study against a control group when there is a common aim for the new and older techniques. Of course there will be features of the LiD program that we will be able to study empirically—dropout rates, the best grade level to begin the program, assessments of the quality of portfolios going forward, the attitudes of students over the years, whether it works better to allow students' choice of topic, etc. But whether it achieves its aims is as complicated to answer as asking whether social studies achieves its aims. In some significant degree its aims are tied up in what we *mean* by becoming educated and what attainments we *value* in the educated person. No empirical test can resolve the question about whether we value what social studies or LiD propose to achieve. We value students learning to think critically about social issues, and reflecting on family life, and learning about other cultures. Do these studies lead to people better able fulfill the requirements of democratic citizenship? Are these studies successful in committing students to democratic citizenship? Are countries that are democratic but don't have social studies less democratic than those that do? Is the size of a country's prison population a mark of how successfully or not social studies is taught? These kinds of questions baffle current empirical methods of research; we have to deal with them as we deal with any matter of value or meaning in our lives.

I'll leave the negative argument like that, because it really doesn't provide a foundation for LiD; it merely points out that it doesn't have and shouldn't be expected to have the kind of basis the question seems to call for; it isn't vulnerable for lacking such a basis. Let us, then, turn to the positive argument. This is dangerous territory because it will open up what I have not been eager to expose too directly, and which will explain why some people immediately respond that the idea is idiotic. It seems idiotic to some for a good reason; it is based on ideas that are at odds with some beliefs that currently dominate educational thinking. And this also accounts for the enthusiastic response of others, because it seems to them to offer a way out of the stranglehold of those ideas. Well, let me dive in at the deep, theoretical, end.

I began with an overview of the set of my books that preceded this one because they lay out the grounds that support LiD. An introductory argument they make is that we can best make sense of the disputes about education today by seeing that current educational thinking is made up of three big ideas, all of which most people hold in varying degrees—and it's the variations in the degree to which people hold the ideas that causes us so much educational strife.

The oldest idea is that the purpose of education is to make the young gradually accommodate to the norms, values, and conventions of adult society. The young are to be equipped with the skills, understandings, beliefs, and so on, that being a successful adult requires. This remains for most people the dominant idea in their concept of education. If a prominent activity of adults is to hunt mastodons or program computers, then the skills of mastodon hunting or computer programming will be justified as components of the curriculum. The criterion for what should go into the school curriculum in this idea is current adult society; the aim of education is to support its continuance and development.

The next oldest idea is that education has to do what is best for the minds of the young. The young are to be taught those things that will most fully develop their mental powers. Many forms of knowledge and artistic pursuits may help to develop youthful minds, even though they may have no particular social utility. The mind, in this view, is shaped and largely constituted by the knowledge it learns, so selection of the best material for the curriculum is most important. The criterion of education in this idea is some ideal conception of the mind; the aim of education is to produce people who embody the most sophisticated cultural attainments who are profoundly knowledgeable about their world and the varieties of human experience.

The third and most recent idea is that the mind is like the body in that it goes through regular stages of development to maturity. The curriculum is to be made up of those experiences that best support students' learning at each stage of the process and carry the process of development forward. But all students' minds are different, and so the curriculum must attend also to each student's individual differences, helping to develop their critical thinking skills and other cognitive, affective, social, political, artistic, spiritual, etc., potentials. Students' own interests and questions should help determine the curriculum. The criterion of education in this idea is a conception of a "natural" or spontaneous developmental process attuned to individual differences; the aim of education is to support this developmental process as fully as possible, bringing each student to as full a realization of individual potential as possible.

These are all important ideas, of course, and they have been hugely influential in shaping educational institutions, methods of teaching, and so on. Indeed, nothing else has been remotely as influential. As J. M. Keynes observed: "Practical people who believe themselves to be quite exempt from any intellectual influences, are usually the slaves of some defunct theorist" (Keynes 1936). That is, the views we think of as our own, forged from our experience and thinking, are for the most part products of dead "academic scribblers" and the ideas they have left behind. We do what we do in education because of the ideas we hold, and the big ideas that have dominated educational thinking and practice are mainly those summarized briefly above. (See Egan 2008 for an extended discussion of them.)

In an ideal view, these three big ideas would slot neatly together, each complementing the others, like three great horses pulling the chariot of education along the curriculum.

The harried educational administrator's job is often seen as balancing the demands of these three big ideas and, in practice, balancing the demands of the interest groups who push for one over the others. The educational administrators are harried because the three big ideas never do seem to slot neatly together in practice—the three horses seem intent on galloping off in different directions, and the great chariot of education seems in constant danger of wreckage. So, for example, the administrator has to try to accommodate those who want more urgent attention, and curriculum time, given to developing early the relevant skills that will prepare students for a competitive job market with those who want a more academic curriculum and a reintroduction of Latin and with those who insist that only by allowing more time for students' free exploration will they ever truly learn anything.

The administrators', and our, problem is that the three big ideas each has inherent in it a different aim for the educational process. We can follow Zvi Lamm and call them "socialization," "acculturation," and "individuation" (Lamm 1976). In the first case the educational process delivers to us a well-socialized person, comfortably embedded in society, accepting its core values and norms of behavior, and well-equipped to earn a living and support the economy. In the second we are delivered with a scholarly person, committed to lifelong learning and to a refined cultural life. The third idea's aim is to produce a psychologically stable person with well-developed interests and involvement in areas of social, artistic, or other enterprises that are tied in with her or his particular and distinctively developed potentials.

Our current system of schooling has been working with the general assumption that we can have it all; that the school can deliver each of these aims. These aims are, after all, merely an abstract reflection of the "mission statements" of virtually every educational institution in the galaxy. All schools promise, or at least aim, to deliver good citizens with "job-ready skills," academic excellence, and the development of each student's individual potential.

LiD among the Competing Ideas

I have elsewhere (1997, 2008) argued that these three ideas are not simply cheerful companions each contributing a share of an adequate education; rather each tends to undermine the other two. They are constant competitors. Now, this is a complex argument made elsewhere, and I don't want to repeat it here, except in as far as it helps to situate LiD. That is, there are features of each of these three ideas that can lead their adherents to support LiD and features of them that are hostile to LiD. Let's try to unwrap them. Each idea also offers some foundation for LiD, even though its main foundation lies elsewhere—which we'll come to later.

The third idea is the most recent and has been perhaps the most potent, particularly undermining the force of the second idea. The common labels applied to these ideas have been "progressivist" (idea no. 3) and "traditionalist" (idea no. 2) forms of education. Many people become a little irritated when such divisions in thinking about education are pointed out, being unable to understand why they can't simply work easily together. Some reflection on why these general aims and means of education have been the central combatants in the curriculum wars for more than a hundred years should help to bring out the scale of the problem in having them work easily together.

Progressivism grew out of dissatisfaction with the traditional curriculum. The belief that teaching a curriculum of what educators thought the most valuable knowledge would shape students' minds in desirable ways seemed increasingly to many an illusion, or at best a hit and miss affair, with more evident misses than hits. Something more was needed than just ensuring the "best" knowledge was learned. No traditionalist, of course, ever believed that simply learning the knowledge by itself would produce the well-educated person, but that became the general caricature of traditional ideas within the rhetoric of progressivists.

That rhetoric is best known still through John Dewey's writings so I will exemplify distinct features of progressivism by quoting from Dewey's "My Pedagogic Creed" (1897) in what follows. We have inherited scorn for the "ornamental" curriculum, which required disciplined study of classical languages and grammar and was seen as interested only in the final product of education and cared little for the process of learning the child had to go through ("I believe that education, therefore, is a process of living and not a preparation for future living," p. 78). The traditionalist methods were seen to rely on force to compel learning of what would thus become "inert" facts; also they were teacher dominated, and the child's activity is thus controlled from without ("The child's own instincts and powers furnish the material and give the starting point for all education. Save as the efforts of the educator connect with some activity which the child is carrying on of his own initiative independent of the educator, education becomes reduced to a pressure from without," p. 77). Students' learning should not be separated from the everyday life of the student because that is what makes so much schooling become remote, dull, and inert ("It should take up and continue the activities with which the child is already familiar in the home," p. 77). Nor are students to be inactive and passive while teachers simply tell them things ("They should be active, [involved in] expressive or constructive activities," p. 78). Also the mind is seen not as simply a repository for any facts teachers might want to "bank" there, but is a living organism that is constantly active and constructive of meaning, and is an organism that goes through its own process of development, of which the educator must be keenly aware ("I believe that the question of method is ultimately reducible to the question of the order of development of the child's powers and interests. The law for presenting and treating material is the law implicit within the child's own nature," p. 78). Students' developing minds are all different, and the teacher must be aware of those differences, as well as their stages of development, in order to present knowledge in a way that students can grasp in a meaningful way ("Without insight into the psychological structure and activities of the individual, the educative process will, therefore, be haphazard and arbitrary. If it chances to coincide with the child's activity it will get a leverage; if it does not, it will result in friction, or disintegration, or arrest of the child nature," p. 77). The child's own interests should be decisive in determining teaching and curriculum ("I believe that interests are the signs and symptoms of growing power. I believe that they represent dawning capacities. Accordingly the constant and careful observation of interests is of the utmost importance for the educator. I believe that these interests are to be observed as showing the state of development which the child has reached," p. 79). Moral education comes not from teaching lessons and sermonizing, but living in genuine communities in democratic classrooms ("Moral training is precisely that which one gets through having to enter into proper relations with others in a unity of work and thought," p. 78).

This is the general view that has prevailed in much thinking about education today. It is worth spelling out a bit here because it may indicate some of the grounds on which some people assume the LiD program is objectionable—i.e., it doesn't fit readily with the presuppositions many have taken from Dewey and other progressivist writers. For example, being randomly assigned a topic like the circus or the solar system may be quite unconnected with what some child "is already familiar with in the home." (Mind you, again, one might wonder how children's common fascination with dinosaurs, monsters, pirates, and wicked witches can be taken as compatible with this fundamental tenet of progressivism.) Also the expectation that students will build their own portfolios working separately, even if they may choose to work with others at various times, runs afoul of the idea that social interactions and a unity of work and thought should be dominant and that the child's own interest should determine what they learn. This helps explains why many people say they would like LiD better if the children could choose their own topics. LiD also emphases learning wholly regardless of "social engagement," and it supports the accumulation of socially pointless knowledge. It also seeks to stimulate expertise dissociated from students' everyday activities, and it involves the imposition of topics from "without"—even if one lets students choose their topic, they would have to choose from among a list predetermined by the criteria outlined earlier.

And yet some progressivists like LiD because some of its features seem compatible with, and adequately based on, other principles of progressivism—they look at LiD and see "active" students pursuing their own interests in a topic in an unconstrained fashion, allowing their individual development and learning style to shape what and how they study. So within the progressivist tradition there are certainly a number of principles that can be used to support introducing LiD to the curriculum, even while other progressivist principles might cause considerable resistance. Whether educators who see themselves as generally committed to progressivism support or resist LiD seems to turn on which of the principles above they value most highly.

Some traditionalists seem to like LiD because it supports the idea of accumulating significant amounts of knowledge and values the attainment of mastery and expertise as a central component of being educated. Even if LiD is a slightly exotic approach to achieving this end, most traditionalists recognize that exploring any topic in depth will eventually expose students to many disciplines and modes of inquiry. Some support it because it does at least imbue what they consider a generally inadequate curriculum with a strand of thorough learning, which might then be able to infect the rest of schooling. That is, they see it as a kind of Trojan horse, breaching the walls of what they consider a progressivism-dominated system.

Especially important for traditionalist support is the belief that knowledge itself shapes the mind. In this view the mind is not like the body in the ways that have become almost a presupposition of modern developmental ideas in education. Traditionalist thinkers tend to believe that the mind does not go through stages of the kind that are taken for granted by so many educators today. They are more inclined to support critics of current developmental ideas. Jerry Fodor, for a prominent example, notes that he is "inclined to doubt that there is such a thing as cognitive development in the sense that developmental cognitive psychologists have in mind" (Fodor 1985, p. 35; see also Fodor 1983), and Rom Harré, for another, claims that there "is no internal schedule of [cognitive] maturation that parallels the internally driven schedule of physical development" (foreword to Morss 1990, p. xii). Their doubts may seem strange to those who simply take it for granted that "cognitive development" is an obvious fact of children's maturation, and that theories like Piaget's describe this process more or less adequately.

It is the old problem that we see the world through the theories we adopt—they serve us like lenses on the world, and after a while we forget we are using lenses or theories and assume we see the world as it is. For example, cognitive developmental theories account for the common appearance of abstract forms of thinking (Piaget's "formal operations," for example) in the mid-teens as a result of a process of "development" —given appropriate interactions with the environment and students' continued learning. That is, these forms of thinking are seen to be driven by a psychological process that needs only certain environmental supports to become realized. The traditionalist account of the same change in students' thinking around mid-teen years is that it is a product of the way knowledge works—when human minds accumulate an adequate amount of knowledge, its growing complexity drives the mind to begin ordering it in new ways. Now, these two accounts may seem similar in that they both rely on minds and knowledge interacting to produce the effect we commonly observe. But to the progressivist this form of thinking is a product of a psychological process primarily, to which knowledge is merely an "aliment," as food is to the growing body; in the traditionalist view this form of abstract thinking is the product of an epistemological process primarily, which requires no supposed psychological developmental process to explain it.

In the *Wrong* book (Egan 2002) I show how Herbert Spencer tied ideas about evolution, development, and progress tightly together. Our modern ideas about developmental psychology inherited a conception of development that was complicatedly tied up with a nineteenth-century conception of progress. As a result, our educational ideas about students' development are "hierarchical integrative"—that is, each stage or phase of development contains, elaborates, and builds on the developments of the previous stage(s). They have the characteristics of progress, and consequently do not observe losses that might be entailed in development. And, as Merlin Donald has convincingly shown, many cognitive changes, both in our cultural history and our individual development, entail losses as well as gains—an idea that is very hard to grasp if one has taken on board the progress-influenced ideas of development from the nineteenth century. As Donald puts it, "high levels of literacy skills may entail considerable costs, as indeed has been suggested by the literature comparing the cognitive competences of oral cultures with those of literate ones. Oral memory and visual imagery are often listed among the skills that may have been traded off against literacy" (Donald 1993, p. 746; see also Donald 1991).

Where is all this going?—you may well ask. I am trying to indicate that we can identify some bases for LiD in, so far, two of the great educational ideas of our time. But it is hardly an uncontentious basis as, particularly in the case of progressivism, LiD is at odds with much that is commonly taken for granted today. LiD might seem to fit more comfortably within general traditionalist conceptions of education and, in return, be supported by them.

One claim of traditionalists is that progressivism has systematically underestimated the value of knowledge itself on the mind's development—the mind is, in this traditionalist view, little more than the knowledge it learns. So, for example, "To acquire knowledge is to learn to see, to experience the world in a way otherwise unknown, and thereby come to have a mind in a fuller sense. It is not that the mind is some kind of organ or muscle with its own inbuilt forms of operation, which if somehow developed, naturally lead to different kinds of knowledge. It is not that the mind has predetermined patterns of functioning" (Hirst 1974, p. 40). In this view, the idea that we can locate and describe, as in Piaget's theory, some underlying process of cognitive development is an illusion. What has been the subject of research on development, Hirst suggests, is simply a by-product of the kind and amount of knowledge students have learned. If there are regularities to be seen, they are produced by the regularities of our teaching students certain forms of knowledge at regular times.

The story so far: We have three great but competing ideas about education and its proper aims. Two of these ideas (no. 2, traditionalism/acculturation, and no. 3, progressivism/individuation) have dominated the verbal battles about education since the founding of the public schools. When it comes to LiD, there are reasons why some who hold to idea no. 3 can find it attractive: LiD encourages active engagement, provides opportunities for uncoerced learning, involves exploration driven by the student's own interests, allows individual learning styles and stages of development free rein in influencing students' research of their topics, and builds students' confidence as learners. But there are also reasons why some progressivists find it objectionable: students are being denied choice of their topic (well, that's not a dogma of LiD, merely a preference of mine—just that the topics must conform with the criteria in chapter 4), they are being "forced" to stick to one topic through twelve years, we don't need this kind of socially useless expertise on random topics, and an approach based on "knowledge for knowledge's sake" has long been discounted as moving students away from real world application of their learning.

Among those who hold idea no. 2, many find LiD attractive because it encourages expertise, gives students insight into the difference between knowledge and opinion, exposes them to the pleasure of learning for its own sake, and significantly enlarges the minds of those who successfully conclude the program. But some traditionalists' interest is muted by LiD's unorganized features—instruction is too casual and students' exploration lacks logical structure; relying on students' interests, the process is too undisciplined.

So within the two major traditions of educational thought, there are some grounds to support LiD and also some grounds to find it objectionable. What I have tried to do so far is identify some bases for LiD within the context of current educational ideas; within both idea no. 2 and idea no. 3 we can find values and meanings of education that give some grounding and support to the LiD program.

The other idea (no. 1, socializing) has persisted as a constant backdrop to the rhetorical battles between the other two ideas. The rhetorical battles often have seemed irrelevant and irritating to the politicians and businesspeople who have primarily an economic and social stake in schooling. Arguments about "discovery techniques" against "didactics" have them chewing the furniture because neither seems to be delivering the basic goods they are paying for—i.e., good citizens with appropriate job skills. But I do also see LiD as offering something important to people whose thinking about schools is dominated by idea no. 1. But showing this involves a step beyond the more familiar realms of current educational discourse, and deals, dangerously, with social virtues, so I will leave this brief discussion of a further basis of LiD to a later section.

A Further Educational Idea

Now while we can discover some bases for the LiD program in some aspects of progressivism and some more within traditionalism, there is a further more substantial basis that the discussion so far is leading toward. To get there I have to confess that when I said that educational thinking has been made up of mixes of three big ideas, I should have said it can increasingly be said to be made up of three-and-a-half ideas.

The half idea, or perhaps the shadow of an idea that is becoming increasingly substantial as a fourth idea, can be understood in the context of the work of Lev Vygotsky (1896–1934)—a psychologist and philosopher who has become quite popular in North America in the past few decades. Vygotsky emphasized the social origins of our thinking, and he showed how the development of our minds is mediated by socioculturally evolved "tools" (see, for example, Vygotsky 1962, 1978, 1997, 1998; Wertsch 1985, 1991, 1997, 1998; Kozulin 1998; Kozulin et al. 2003).

In Vygotsky's view, contrary to Piaget's theories, learning and using cognitive tools drives the developmental process, particularly by the way in which the cultural tools generated in our history are picked up by students today and become cognitive tools for them. Actually it's not so much that knowledge drives development—which suggests some common developmental process and you can choose whether you prefer knowledge or some psychological process as the driver—but rather that the accumulation of cognitive tools *is* development. So, for example, over centuries people learned to make maps as tools for helping us to find our way around. The cultural tool, or set of tools, that constitute mapmaking and map reading today can be learned by students and become for them cognitive tools. So cultural tools can be internalized and transformed into cognitive tools. From a Vygotskian point of view, for example, students do not internalize concepts or knowledge directly, which is the view that tends to be common in idea no. 2, nor do they construct their knowledge on the basis of their own experience, which is a common view in idea no. 3.

The implications of what may seem somewhat arcane theoretical differences are, for education, very significant. The aim of education in this idea no. 4 is to maximize for students the array of cultural tools they acquire and transform into cognitive tools. The greater an individual's cognitive tool kit, the fuller and richer sense he or she can make of the world and experience. These "tools" are a somewhat different category from any we are used to in thinking about education, and yet they are the category that is central to a Vygotsky-oriented theory of education.

Despite the attempts to absorb Vygotsky to progressivism and to Piagetian ideas (DeVries 2000), his theory is profoundly at odds with the "biologized mind" (Sugarman 1987; Morss 1990) of modern Western developmental psychology. In Vygotsky's view, the mind is in significant degree composed by its accumulation of cognitive tools. It is a view that shares more with Paul Hirst's claim above than it does with the prevailing beliefs about the regular unfolding of an internal schedule of developmental stages, while, of course, being also different in some regards from Hirst's image of the elaboration of mind.

For Vygotky, the cultural/cognitive tools students can learn and put to work are tied in with the cultural content in which they were given birth or find richest use. That is, the development of cognitive tools is tied in with learning a great deal of one's cultural heritage. So Kozulin describes works of Shakespeare, Tolstoy, and other literary giants as producing "higher-order" tools or "super-tools" for stimulating a wide range of cognitive developments (1998, chap. 6); learning to follow Shakespeare's language and poetry, sympathizing with the range of his characters and their emotions, imagining with him the complex relationships he sets in place, and so on, all—to echo Hirst's terms—leads to our having a fuller, richer, more comprehensive mind. On a simpler scale, learning to read maps or solve an equation in algebra or prove a theorem in geometry provide more utilitarian tools, whereas learning to master the subjunctive is a more versatile tool, but all of them serve to enlarge our minds.

My earlier books constitute an attempt to rethink education, teaching, learning, and the school, and so contribute to this idea no. 4. I have tried to articulate in terms suitable for education the most powerful sets of cognitive tools whose development can form a better basis for an educational program than those that have been generated from progressive or traditional educational theories. So I have described the major sense-making tool kits available to us as, first, our bodies (which deliver what I call somatic understanding), with their senses, emotions, humor, patterning, musicality, intentional gesturing, etc., then the development of oral language (mythic understanding), and such "tools" as recognizing and shaping events and characters into stories, forming images from words, metaphor recognition and construction, rhyme and rhythm, binary structuring, etc., then the mastery of literacy (romantic understanding), and such "tools" as engagement by extremes and limits, associations with the heroic, sense of wonder, narrative understanding, collecting and hobbies, etc., then of theoretic thinking (philosophic understanding), and such "tools" as the sense of abstract reality, social agency, general ideas and their anomalies, search for abstract truth and authority, meta-narratives, etc., and finally of highly reflexive irony (ironic understanding). Put so starkly, of course, this will look a tad bizarre. What it suggests, though, is a crucial way in which idea no. 4 is different from its predecessors, and which leads us back to LiD.

Idea no. 4 does not see the accumulation of privileged knowledge in disciplined structures as forming the educated mind, as does idea no. 2, nor does it see students' interests and exploration shaping a curriculum whose purpose is to support a putative developmental process, as does idea no. 3. Yet idea no. 4 does greatly value the importance of accumulating knowledge, because cognitive tools are always tied to knowledge. These tools are not disembodied skills one might master, or learn how to learn; they are products of learning specific knowledge in specific conditions. And idea no. 4 greatly values students' own exploration and individual interests, but it recognizes that they can become educationally important only if they are realized within the acquisition of logically and psychologically constrained sequences of cognitive tool acquisition, which stimulate the imagination.

So LiD does have some basis in idea no. 2 and also in idea no. 3, but it comes into its own as ensuring both the accumulation of knowledge and also stimulation of students' exploration determined by their own interests when these are both constrained and enlarged by the sequences of cognitive tool acquisition briefly mentioned above, and elaborated in chapter 5. That is, education, in idea no. 4, is neither the internalization of disciplined knowledge in logical sequences nor development through a sequence of genetically predetermined stages fed by knowledge, but is a process shaped by logical and psychological constraints evident both in our cultural history and the tool kits that that history has delivered to us. I have described this process, even if in a somewhat inadequate way, in the sequence of kinds of understanding sketched above and described in more detail in Egan 1997. These are the principles that show how LiD is not merely an amassing of bits of knowledge but is rather a supertool for the systematic development of a sequence of kinds of understanding. As such it finds a significant basis as a method for realizing idea no. 4 in the lives of students.

The Further, Dangerous, Step

I mentioned that LiD can also find some further distinct support within idea no. 1. It has, that is to say, value as a social utility and a contributor to socially important virtues. This is a dangerous step, because it takes us even further into the complex realm of values and meanings.

Some time ago Plato suggested that learning particular forms of knowledge in an appropriate way did not lead only to an accumulated mass of knowledge but could have the effect of turning the soul toward a more virtuous life. The fifty-year program he prescribed to achieve this purpose has not proven to be many people's cup of tea, and attempts to implement in schools the notion that learning can make a person more virtuous has rarely produced the kind of "guardians" he desired for his *Republic*. While no one believes that simply accumulating knowledge can deliver a more virtuous person, the general idea that there might be some connection between accumulating knowledge and attaining virtue seems to be an argument that most of the educational world has given up on. I think educators have given up on Plato's insight too quickly, and the LiD proposal ties together learning something in depth with the cultivation of virtues important in modern society. LiD will involve each student in intensive and extensive exploration, classification, analysis, and experiments, but it will also face them with more than purely intellectual challenges.

To see what I mean when I say that the students' relationship to, and understanding of the nature of, knowledge will be transformed it is helpful to try to imagine students' engagement with their portfolios after ten or eleven years. They will not only have learned a great deal, but they will have classified and reclassified the knowledge they have learned, they will have pursued aesthetic, medicinal, historical, ethical, etc., dimensions of their topic. (The student who is given the topic of apples, as we have seen, will learn about the varieties of apples, their historical source and development, the current dispersion of varieties around the world, market conditions, ethical concerns with market forces driving reduced variety cultivation, apples in art and stories, the nutritional value of apples, etc.) Mostly they will have begun to become expert. Today students remain, as it were, outside all the knowledge they learn; they learn too little about anything to feel on the "inside" of it. In particular, this slowly accumulating expertise leads to an understanding not of how much one knows but of how much there is to know and how little one has so far mastered. Learning is indeed one of those enterprises in which we come to recognize, like Tennyson's Ulysses, that it "is an arch wherethrough / Gleams that untraveled world, whose margin fades / For ever and for ever when I move." The first virtue the LiD program is designed to encourage, then, is a form of humility.

A second set of social virtues may be identified by contrast with the current norm of students' superficial learning, which leaves them too often vulnerable to being unable to distinguish precisely between knowledge and opinion, which in turn generates forms of solipsism and lack of critical reflection that are socially and individually destructive. Their antonyms will be among the virtues I anticipate the LiD program encouraging: students who follow the LiD program will be less vulnerable to persuasion by advertisers, politicians, and others who do not distinguish well between knowledge and what they would like to believe, and, more important, LiD students will be open to self-doubt, hold judgments and beliefs in abeyance till appropriate evidence has been brought to bear on issues, and, in general, develop a commitment to discovering and holding to the truth in whatever degree possible. Even if, as A. E. Housman suggested, "the faintest of all human passions is the love of truth" (1961, p. 43), it is the virtue that Plato

believed central to an educated person and a civilized state. (I recognize that "truth" is a deeply contentious term at the moment,
and use it here as an abbreviation for a commitment to what we
can find more reliable grounds for believing.)

LiD, then, is not only a program designed to enlarge students'
cognition; it also has the potential to move students in the direction Plato recommended for an educational program, by encouraging them even if hesitatingly and in a small way for most students,
in the direction of such virtues as humility and a commitment to
truth. What form the ancient virtue of humility might take in an
innovative program designed to encourage development of expertise about, say, apples, dust, or the circus, remains to be seen. But
while this claim on virtue might seem to many like extravagant
hyperbole, and evidence that the writer has exposed finally the
extent of his nuttiness, I mention it not to stake any claim that
this will be a common product of the program, but simply because
if I am listing the supports of LiD, one of them is related to an old
argument of Plato's. And in arguments about education it is hard
to think of a sturdier ally.

Conclusion

Far from being a baseless idea, LiD can be seen as supported by
some aspects of all the main ideas that have dominated educational thinking for the last couple of centuries and as contributing something to each of them. It is based more firmly on, and
contributes more fully to, a sociocultural/cultural-recapitulation
theory that can be seen as articulating in a somewhat new way
a Vygotskian conception of education. These bases in turn rest
on what we value as components of an educated person and on
what we mean by education. I have tried to spell out some meanings of education that give support to putting LiD into practice in
schools. Even though idea no. 4 offers the best basis and the most
convincing reasons for implementing LiD, there seem enough
reasons in the other three ideas to expect LiD to serve as a useful
contributor to their aims.

While LiD appears to some people, at least on first acquaintance, as concerned only with accumulating knowledge in a traditionalist fashion, it might be useful to conclude this appendix with a reminder that it grew out of a long research program focused on how to engage students' emotions and imagination in the content of the curriculum. I have tried to separate the kind of engagement one might expect to see in students with their LiD topics from that one may see involved in children's hobbies or collections. Certainly there is likely to be some overlap between the two, especially during the years from around eight to fourteen, but hobbies and collections are appropriate to bear in mind as demonstrating that a kind of obsessive engagement with something is quite common for nearly all children—it's just that we don't see it happen in school very much. This leads those who see children mainly in schools to fail to recognize that students becoming keenly engaged with their portfolios on *apples* or *dust* or *beetles* is not at all unlikely if only we create the conditions for it to become realized..

An underlying principle that I drew from the work on Imaginative Education (www.icrg.net) is that all knowledge is human knowledge—that is, all knowledge is a product of someone's hopes, fears, or passions, and if we hope to engage students' interests, we have to show knowledge in the context of the hopes, fears, and passions that generated it in the first place or that give it a living meaning today. Unfortunately, so much of the content of the curriculum is routinely taught as though its natural habitat is a textbook rather than the fears, hopes, and passions of real people that students too commonly find it dull and lifeless, and unengaging. And partly that is a product of making the curriculum into a kind of encyclopedia of all the knowledge we would like students to learn, but we have done it in such a way that students make only superficial contact with most of it, and hardly ever learn in the context of the hopes and fears and passions that alone can make knowledge live.

One purpose of the slow accumulation of knowledge about any of these LiD topics is to ensure that no student will stop with the superficial knowledge that fills most of the curriculum currently, but that all students will be drawn on to learn about the people who established the knowledge—who propagated apple varieties, who discovered the life cycle of dust mites, who came to love beetles in all their astonishing variety, and so on.

It is useful to remember that there is no knowledge in a library; there is no knowledge on the Internet. We forget too easily our great ingenuity in coding knowledge into symbols, and we then forget that the codes are not knowledge, but only cunning reminders of knowledge. Knowledge exists only in living human tissue, in our brains. And the hard trick of education is to transform the codes and symbols into living knowledge. If one fails to recognize the difference, then of course one will fail to understand that a further transformational step is essential for adequate education. In an educational world driven by assessment procedures that accept as success the ability of students to replicate the codes and symbols they have learned, there is no incentive to ensure that students manage the crucial transformational act of bringing the symbols to new life in new minds. What we have then—what we have too commonly now—is a parody of education. LiD is designed to bring knowledge to life in a way that will encourage something of genuine educational value for all the students who become involved in the program.

Appendix B

A Brief Outline of the

Learning in Depth Program

The Learning in Depth program (LiD) is designed as an additional contribution schools can make to students' education. Though relatively simple, it has the potential to make a major impact. The aim is to build knowledge, understanding, skills, and practices fundamental to effective learning.

The Basic Idea

In the first week of schooling, each student will be randomly assigned a topic to learn in depth. The topics might be such things as birds, apples, the circus, railways, the solar system, etc. Each student will then study his or her assigned topic until grade 12, along with the usual curriculum. Students will meet regularly with their supervising teachers, who will give guidance, suggestions, and help as students build personal portfolios on their topics. The aim is that each student, by the end of her or his schooling, will develop genuine expertise about that topic. The project proposes—and draws on what research is available to suggest—that this process of learning in depth has the potential to transform the schooling experience of nearly all children by transforming their relationship to, and understanding of the nature of, knowledge.

Some Potential Benefits of LiD

For students: Provides knowledge of some topic in great breadth and depth; gives a deep understanding of the nature of knowledge; engages students' imaginations and emotions in learning; builds confidence; builds expertise in use of Internet and organizational skills.

For teachers: Teachers discover along with students; no pressures to grade and assess; working with enthusiastic learners; students' depth knowledge will enrich regular teaching.

For the school: Provides a means for older and younger students to cooperate in learning; makes the school into a center of expertise on many topics; enriches the culture of the school; displays of topics will provide attractive focus of attention.

This proposal for a new element of the curriculum is based on the belief that learning something in depth will add an important dimension to each person's education. It is further based on the principle that the more one knows about anything, the more interesting it becomes.

Imaginative Education Research Group:
www.ierg.net/LiD

References

Ashton-Warner, Sylvia. 1972. *Spearpoint: Teacher in America*. New York: Knopf.

Atran, Scott, and Douglas Medin. 2009. *The native mind and the cultural construction of nature*. Cambridge, MA: MIT Press.

Barrows, Thomas S., Stephen F. Klein, John D. Clark, and Nathanial Hartshorne. 1981. *College students' knowledge and beliefs: A survey of global understanding*. The Final Report of the Global Understanding Project. Educational Testing Service. New Rochelle, NY: Change Magazine Press.

Bauerlein, Mark. 2008. *The dumbest generation: How the digital age stupefies young Americans and jeopardizes our future (or, Don't trust anyone under 30)*. New York: Jeremy P. Tarcher/Penguin.

Bettelheim, Bruno. 1976. *The uses of enchantment*. New York: Knopf.

Bruner, Jerome. 1960. *The process of education*. Cambridge, MA: Harvard University Press.

———. 1988. Discussion. *Yale Journal of Criticism* 2 (1).

Chall, Jeanne. 2002. *The academic achievement challenge: What really works in the classroom?* New York: Guilford Press.

Conklin, Harold. 1955. The relationship of Hanunoo agriculture to the plant world. Ph.D. thesis, Yale University.

Cremin, Lawrence A. 1955. The revolution in American secondary education, 1893–1918. *Teachers College Record* 56 (March).

DeVries, Rheta. 2000. Vygotsky, Piaget, and education: A reciprocal assimilation of theories and educational practices. *New Ideas in Psychology* 18, no. 2–3 (August): 187–213.

Dewey, John. 1897. My pedagogic creed. *School Journal* 54: 77–80.

———. 1966. *Democracy and education.* New York: Free Press. (First published, 1916.)

Donald, Merlin. 1991. *Origins of the modern mind.* Cambridge, MA: Harvard University Press.

———. 1993. Précis of *Origins of the modern mind:* Three stages in the evolution of culture and cognition. *Behavioral and Brain Sciences* 16, no. 4 (December): 737–91.

Egan, Kieran. 1988. *Primary understanding: Education in early childhood.* New York: Routledge.

———. 1990. *Romantic understanding: The development of rationality and the imagination, ages 8–15.* New York: Routledge.

———. 1997. *The educated mind: How cognitive tools shape our understanding.* Chicago: University of Chicago Press.

———. 2002. *Getting it wrong from the beginning: Our progressivist inheritance from Herbert Spencer, John Dewey, and Jean Piaget.* New Haven, CT: Yale University Press.

———. 2008. *The future of education: Reimagining the school from the ground up.* New Haven, CT: Yale University Press.

Fodor, Jerry. 1983. *The modularity of mind.* Cambridge, MA: MIT Press.

———. 1985. Précis of *The modularity of mind. Behavioral and Brain Sciences* 8: 1–42.

Francis, Mark. 2007. *Herbert Spencer and the invention of modern life.* Ithaca, NY: Cornell University Press.

Gardner, Howard. 1999. *The disciplined mind: What all students should understand.* New York: Simon and Schuster.

Gardner, Howard, and Ellen Winner. 1979. The development of metaphoric competence: Implications for humanistic disciplines. In *On metaphor,* ed. Sheldon Sacks. Chicago: University of Chicago Press.

Gay, Hannah. 1998. No "Heathen's Corner" here: The failed campaign to memorialize Herbert Spencer in Westminster Abbey. *British Journal of the History of Science* 31: 41–54.

Havelock, Eric. 1963. *Preface to Plato.* Cambridge, MA: Harvard University Press.

———. 1986. *The Muse learns to write.* New Haven, CT: Yale University Press.

Hirst, Paul. 1974. *Knowledge and the curriculum.* London: Routledge and Kegan Paul.

Housman, A. E. 1961. *The name and nature of poetry and other selected prose.* Ed. John Carter. Cambridge: Cambridge University Press.

Innis, Harold. 1951. *The bias of communication.* Toronto: University of Toronto Press.

Katz, Lilian G., and Sylvia C. Chard. 1989. *Engaging children's minds: The project approach.* Norwood, NJ: Ablex Publishing.

———. 1998a. *The project approach: Developing the basic framework. Practical guide 1 and 2.* New York: Scholastic.

———. 1998b. Issues in selecting topics for projects. ERIC Digest, EDO-PS-98-8. http://ceep.crc.uiuc.edu/eecearchive/digests/1998/katzpr98.pdf.

Keynes, John Maynard. 1936. *General theory of employment, interest and money.* London: Macmillan.

Kilpatrick, Thomas H. 1918. The project method. *Teachers College Record* 19: 319–34.

Knoll, Michael. 1995. The project method: Its origin and international influence. In *Progressive education across the continents: A handbook,* ed. Volker Lenhart and Hermann Röhrs. New York: Lang.

Kozulin, Alex. 1998. *Psychological tools: A sociocultural approach to education.* Cambridge, MA: Harvard University Press.

Kozulin, Alex, Boris Gindis, Vladimir S. Ageyev, and Suzanne M. Miller, eds. 2003. *Vygotsky's educational theory in context.* Cambridge: Cambridge University Press.

Lamm, Zvi. 1976. *Conflicting theories of instruction: Conceptual dimensions.* Berkeley, CA: McCutchan.

Lévi-Strauss, Claude. 1966. *The savage mind.* Chicago: University of Chicago Press.

Morss, John R. 1990. *The biologising of childhood: Developmental psychology and the Darwinian myth.* Hove, East Sussex: Erlbaum.

National Commission on Excellence in Education. 1983. *A nation at risk: The imperative for educational reform.* Washington, DC: Government Printing Office.

Ong, Walter. 1982. *Orality and literacy.* London: Methuen.

Peters, Richard, and Paul Hirst. 1970. *The logic of education.* London: Routledge and Kegan Paul.

Postman, Neil, and Charles Weingartner. 1971. *Teaching as a subversive activity.* New York: Delta.

Sugarman, Susan. 1987. *Piaget's construction of the child's reality.* Cambridge: Cambridge University Press.

Tanner, Daniel, and Laura N. Tanner. 1980. *Curriculum development: Theory into practice.* 2nd ed. New York: Macmillan.

Vygotsky, Lev. 1962. *Thought and language.* Trans. Eugenia Haufmann and Gertrude Vakar. Cambridge, MA: MIT Press.

———. 1978. *Mind in society: The development of higher psychological processes.* Ed. Michael Cole, Vera John-Steiner, and Sylvia Scribner Cambridge, MA: Harvard University Press.

———. 1997. *The history of the development of higher mental functions.* Ed. Robert W. Rieber, Marie J. Hall, and Joseph Glick. Volume 4 of *The collected works of L. S. Vygotsky.* Ed. R. W. Rieber and A. S. Carton. New York: Plenum.

———. 1998. *Child psychology.* Ed. Robert W. Rieber and Marie J. Hall. Volume 5 of *The collected works of L. S. Vygotsky.* Ed. R. W. Rieber and A. S. Carton. New York: Plenum.

Webb, Beatrice. 1926. *My apprenticeship.* London: Longmans, Green, and Co.

Wertsch, James V. 1985. *Vygotsky and the social formation of mind.* Cambridge, MA: Harvard University Press.

———. 1991. *Voices of the mind: A sociocultural approach to mediated action.* Cambridge, MA: Harvard University Press.

———. 1997. *Mind as action.* New York: Oxford University Press.

———. 1998. Mediated action. In *A companion to cognitive science,* ed. William Bechtel and George Graham. Oxford: Blackwell.